GARFIELD
THE MOVIE

Novelization by H. S. Newcomb

**Based on the screenplay written by
Joel Cohen and Alec Sokolow**

Based on the character created by

BALLANTINE BOOKS
NEW YORK

Photography: Gemma La Mana

Color bonus section:

Writers
Scott Nickel, Mark Acey

Designer
Betsy Knotts

www.ballantinebooks.com

Library of Congress Control Number: 2004090365

ISBN 0-345-46908-9

Manufactured in the United States of America

First Edition: May 2004

10   9   8   7   6   5   4   3

Chapter One

In a snug little bed, situated in a modest two-bedroom house on a tiny plot in a sleepy little suburban community, a mound of golden fur slept snugly. Content in the love and obedience of the man sawing wood just one bed away, the fat, happy cat snored and dreamed . . .

He was in a large, elegant room abuzz with the tinkle of stemware and laughter. Every now and then an orchestra struck up a tune. Beautiful women parading a dizzying array of sparkle and feathers sat side by side with impossibly short, rich men called "producers," who were not at all beautiful but paid thousands of dollars for the table.

Dressed to the nine lives in black tie, his bow tie just a bit crooked, the suave orange tabby leaned slowly into the woman seated to his right at the banquet table. She was as beautiful as any girl he'd ever seen . . . dewy and fresh-faced with wide-set brown eyes and sparkling white teeth. She seemed a vision in a pale pink gown, her lips reflecting the color of the roses bursting with life at the center of the table. If anything, she was prettier in person than she was on the big screen, with warm chestnut

1

hair that reflected the soft candlelight flickering amid the flowers.

The tabby brushed a breadcrumb from his cummerbund and inched closer, ears forward, tail swishing in breathless anticipation.

Excuse me, Jennifer, love . . . are you going to eat that?

With one smooth, gulping leap, the cat scarfed the lasagna from her plate, returned to his seat, and proceeded to lick himself as if nothing had happened. You da mannnnn, Stan. He smacked the last of the sauce from his whiskers. She can have my brussels sprouts if she likes.

Suddenly, confusion broke out at the table. The beautiful woman in the pink gown threw her hands together and cried, "Garfield, that's you!" as she smooshed him on the head. Other voices chimed in. "Get up there, Garfield! They're calling your name!" urged a smiling, mild-looking young man seated across from the dapper feline.

I won? Of course I won. Garfield adjusted his tie and trotted to the podium amid a cheering crowd, practicing his acceptance speech on the way. First I'd like to thank the A-cat-emy, and all my worshipping fans, but mostly I want to thank the man without whom none of this would be possible, that born loser and Saturday night special, Jon Arbuckle, who basks in the glory of my light . . .

Speech rehearsed, Garfield leapt onto the podium and turned to face the audience. The spotlight seared over the heads of the audience and straight to the back of his brain. The applause swelled to a deafening roar. He slammed his eyes shut against the light as his bow tie popped from around his neck and fur stuck straight out

*at every angle. He sat before the bright, thundering
crowd, speechless for perhaps the first time in his life.*

Back in the snug little bed, Garfield slowly opened one
eye, only to slam it shut against the rising sun pouring
through the window. As he struggled toward conscious-
ness, the thunderous applause became the grating buzz of
an alarm clock. 7:23 A.M. Garfield swiped a paw, putting an
end to the torture and the dream. *I'd like morning better if
it started later.*

He yawned and looked over at the big bed, where Jon Arbuckle slept soundly in bright red-and-white-striped pajamas. Garfield and his human went back many years, all
the way to the kitchen of Mama Leone's Italian restaurant.
It was there that the ginger tabby came into this world at a
whopping five pounds, six ounces, adopted a short while
later by the eager young bachelor who fled the farm to
make his mark in the big suburb. Weaned on the table
scraps of one of the finest local restaurants, Garfield immediately set about educating Jon to his unusual gastronomic
demands. The early training was a resounding success, for
in no time at all Garfield had Jon just where he wanted
him: dishing up the lasagna and brewing the coffee strong
enough to sit up and bark. As Jon's career grew over time,
so did Garfield's waistline and the love and companionship between man and beast. Now Jon was a successful
freelance cartoonist and a lonely single, and Garfield still
had Jon doing tricks.

He bid good morning to his best friend Pooky, the stuffed
bear Garfield had rescued from the bottom of Jon's dresser
many years ago. Pooky was an excellent listener who was
there whenever Garfield needed him. He never competed

for food or Jon's attention, and was always willing to relinquish the remote control. No one knew Garfield's secrets, hopes, and fears the way Pooky did, not even Jon. And Pooky wasn't telling, mostly because he had no mouth.

"Cover me, Pooky, I'm going in." Garfield delicately stretched a hind paw to test the floor temperature, then jumped from his miniature bed and crossed the room. He padded past the photographs and memories that make a house a home. Here was a snapshot of him dragging Jon from the ski lodge by his bootlace, after the last of the eligible young ladies refused his offer of cocoa. Halloween, the year Jon dressed as a giant mouse. Next to it was a picture from their never-to-be-repeated camping trip, a miserable week of nature punctuated by a total lack of television. Still, Jon was a good man, if overly geeky, and it was a good life.

Jon had failed to respond to the alarm and snored away, rattling the miniblinds. This would never do. If Garfield had to be awake, then Jon should have been showered and preparing the morning meal by now. The cat slithered to the head of the big bed and pulled back the covers, revealing the noisy object of his affection.

Rise and shine, Jon. Time to feed the cat.

The object of Garfield's affection stirred and muttered, "Not *now*, Garfield," and dropped back to sleep, reaching up and pulling the cat into a warm, contented hug. Garfield's ears flattened and his eyes narrowed into slits.

We play this game every morning. I'm a cat. You're my master. You need to lead. You need to provide. You need to get up, *Jon. You're sleeping your life away.*

Jon turned and drew the covers up around his neck, babbling softly about needing a few more minutes. With a

4

dreamy smile on his face, he took a deep breath and squeezed the soft, warm cat closer. Garfield scrunched up his face and began a slow burn. He wriggled from Jon's arms and leapt to a dresser next to the bed, casually knocking over photos, cologne, and an odd little array of golf tees on his way.

I don't think you grasp the severity of the situation, Jon. There is no snooze button on a cat that wants breakfast. I get cranky when I'm hungry. He assumed the position, arms raised, back extended. Wiggling his butt ever so slightly, Garfield calculated the effort-to-distance ratio that lay between him and breakfast. Suddenly Garfield lurched from the dresser like an Acapulco cliff diver, in a clean arch dead-centered on Jon's solar plexus. *Oooof!*

He thrust his face an inch from Jon's nose and stared hard. *And guess what, Jon—I'm ALWAYS hungry!*

In one swift movement Jon sat upright and his eyes sprang open, bugging with a glassy sort of surprise. He yawned, rubbed his face, and glanced at the clock.

"It's seven twenty-three! I forgot to set the alarm! Guess I was up too late last night with the model railroad. Thanks, Garfield. I owe you one!"

Put it on my tabby.

John swung his legs around the side of the bed and wiggled his toes, scratching and searching for his slippers. They were hard to miss, what with their long ears up front and the fluffy cottontails at the ankles.

He slid into his robe, a blue velour with I ❤ MY CAT stitched over the breast pocket, and shuffled toward the bathroom. "Looks like another beautiful morning, Garfield. And there's nothing I like better than to start my day off squeaky clean!"

GARFIELD

Garfield watched Jon's retreat from the bed, completely unamused. *Well, there's nothing I like better than to start my day off fed. Come, Jon. Only I can smell you from here. Breakfast. NOW.*

Jon stepped into the bathroom and turned the spigots, humming cheerfully to himself and adjusting the water until it was just the right temperature. Steam began to fill the room. Garfield followed and sat next to the commode, himself steaming, as Jon stepped into the shower and drew the curtain. The humming grew into full-throttle singing: "I've gotta be meeeee! I've gotta be meeee!"

Yeah, and I've gotta be me.

Staring intently at the caterwauling lump scrubbing himself behind the curtain, Garfield casually lifted a paw and—*whoosh!*—flushed the toilet.

Jon's screams could be heard five houses away.

I am one hot kitty.

Jon stuck his dripping head out from behind the shower curtain and said through gritted teeth, "Breakfast will be served in just a moment."

Moments later, Garfield sat in the kitchen window, sipping a mug of strong, hot coffee while he watched Jon lay out a plate of corned beef hash. *Ohhhh, that smells good. A little mustard on the side would be nice. Is there any rye bread in the house?*

"The day is young, Garfield, and we should make the most of it. How do you feel about doing some exercise this morning?" Jon set the plate on the kitchen table and opened the cupboard.

How do you feel about bleeding this morning?

"It'll do you some good. We can do my Pilates video together."

Too trendy, and I don't really have the time, Jon. You don't have the rigorous napping obligations I do.

"At the rate your tummy is growing, you could make a fortune selling shade," Jon said, casting a hard eye upon Garfield's girth. "Might be the first contribution you make to this household."

Oh, really? And just whose midsection keeps the hardwood floors around here freshly buffed, hmm?

Jon's attention returned to the stack of silver tins in the cabinet. "Let's see . . . 'Salmon Surprise' . . . 'Beef-Bacon Boogie-Woogie' . . . 'Mystery Mélange' . . . Let's try something new this morning, Garfield. Yes, here we go . . . 'Liver-Flavored.' You're going to love it." Jon popped the can of Kibbly Kat, prepared a plate, and set it beside his own on the kitchen table.

As Jon turned his back to recycle the empty can, Garfield sprang into action with an impish smile.

"I know what we could do today," Jon said, as he took his seat and spread a napkin on his lap. "I've noticed you scratching a bit lately. Maybe we should take a drive to see Liz. You like Liz." He lifted the fork to his mouth. "Liz is really an excellent . . ."

Ptuhyee!! Jon spit the food from his mouth as Garfield lapped up the last of the corned beef hash.

"*Liver???*" Jon grimaced and ran for the sink, where he rinsed out his mouth a dozen times and drank a quart of water.

Actually, it's liver-flavored.

7

Chapter Two

After breakfast, Jon and Garfield went into the office, where one flipped on the computer and the other curled up on a sunny windowsill and settled in for a nap. Jon started each workday by checking his daily task organizer. "Let's see, what have I got down for today . . . search Internet for new disco CDs, brainstorm branding project, finish Mom's macramé . . . Hey! What's this? 'Nap'? 'Eat'? 'Hack up hairball'?' Garfield!!! Have you been playing with my computer again?"

Garfield sat on the windowsill and began to wash himself furiously.

Nothing says "I love you, Jon" like a well-placed hairball.

Jon sighed and turned his attention to his latest freelance gig. He sat at his desk, thinking aloud. "Inspiration. That's what I need. There's a new start-up company in town, Garfield, and if I can come up with a really great idea I'll land the account. They're selling in-ground sprinkler systems called 'Showers of Power.' What would make a catchy logo for sprinklers? Maybe something with flowers, since it rhymes." Jon started sketching on his computer. As he reached for the mouse, one of the furry kind skittered past the keyboard.

THE MOVIE

"Eeek! A mouse! Get him, Garfield!"

You get him, Jon.

"Garfie-e-e-e-l-d!" Jon grabbed a broom and started chasing the mouse as it scurried into the living room. *Crash! Thump! Bang!* Jon flailed wildly at the intruder, taking down a lamp, a vase, and two Hummel figurines.

Garfield yawned. *Oh, good. I always hated those things.* He closed his eyes and assumed the sleeping position on the windowsill as Jon continued to hack away at the speedy little rodent, who darted into the kitchen.

The mouse ran back through the office right past Garfield, who had now roused himself to take in the proceedings. *Jon chasing a mouse with a broom and destroying half the house in the process. Where can you get more value for your entertainment buck these days?* He heard Jon ranting in the other room. *Here comes the big finish.*

Jon stumbled after the mouse, stubbing his toe on the frame of the office doorway. *"AHHHH!"* he screamed, writhing in pain. He grabbed his injured foot and hopped up and down on the other, losing his balance and falling backward into the desk. He conked his head on the way down. "Eee-*yow*!" he cried, as he rolled around on the floor in the fetal position. The mouse disappeared.

Ever think of joining the circus, Jon? I hear Bozo's retired.

Jon winced and shot a look at the orange blob sunning himself in the window. "What good is a cat that doesn't chase a mouse??"

Hey, I'm a lover, not a mouser. Besides, I've been working way too hard lately. I'm thinking of subcontracting the shedding.

With that and a great flourish of tail, Garfield slipped out the kitty door and onto the front porch, where the mouse skittered across the boards, turned a corner, and ran smack into the waiting orange cat. Defeated, the trapped rodent smiled sheepishly.

"What are you doing in the house again, Louis? I thought we discussed this." With one paw, Garfield held Louis down by his tail.

"I couldn't help it, Garfield. Jon's got those yummy macadamia nut cookies I like so much . . ."

"Listen to me, Louis. Jon sees you, he expects more from me. You've got to lay low. Take a powder for a week or two. I'll make sure there's a cookie waiting for you."

Louis tugged at his tail, trying in vain to extract it from the ample weight of Garfield's paw. "Garfield, c'mon."

Garfield lowered his head to look Louis straight in his beady little eye. "Louis, as much as it would give me the winds, I *will* eat you." He ran his tongue over his whiskers for emphasis. "Now, you know the drill."

Garfield lifted his paw and Louis hopped into Garfield's open jaw. The cat sauntered into the backyard, where Jon sat rubbing his big toe and thinking about in-ground sprinkler systems. At once he noticed the skinny tail dangling from the ginger cat's mouth.

"I *knew* you could do it once you put your mind to it! You're the best cat any guy could hope to have!" Jon bent down to give Garfield an appreciative pat on the head and then ducked back inside. Garfield dropped Louis immediately.

Blecchhh. Show me a mouser, and I'll show you a cat with bad breath.

Louis tumbled and shook himself back to reality. "Remember, Garfield . . ."

"I know, I know. Macadamia nut cookies. A deal's a deal."

Louis disappeared into the wilds of the cul-de-sac. Garfield stretched. *The day's still young and I'm already in debt. Oh, well. So much time. So little to do. I think I shall now survey my empire.* Garfield rounded the house and walked past the flowering shrubs fronting the porch. The path to the sidewalk was short and flanked by a lush green lawn. Garfield paused on the walkway to chew some blades of grass before arriving at one of the two small boulders at the end of the path.

The King of the Jungle peels off from the pride and trots through the high grass of the Serengeti, ever watchful. The lion settles on the high rock and—"Meow!"—lets out a throaty roar. From this perch he can see for miles over the rolling plains of the vast savanna. The lionesses and their cubs, dependent on the mighty lion for safety, escape the midday sun by curling up under an umbrella tree a hundred yards away. A stranger approaches. Suddenly, the lion's senses are on full alert and a low rumble escapes from deep within him.

"Mornin', Garfield!" chirped a squeaky little voice from below. "Nice day, isn't it?"

Garfield looked down to see an ant crawling up the side of his rock.

"What's the latest, Adam?" he yawned, addressing the ant.

"New spiderweb under construction between the Osborne and Ziccardi houses. You might want to check it out, Garfield. Looks like it's meant to accommodate a really big squishy one."

"Thanks, Adam. I'll try to fit it into my schedule."

Garfield hopped up and continued on his way, passing

one tidy home on top of another. As he approached the Olshan house he slowed, keeping an eye out for the enormous lady who lived there. Garfield liked this Olshan
woman so much more before she got fat. In her thinner days
she would often stoop to scratch his head while she trimmed
her hedges or swept the driveway. But now rumor had it that
she was expecting a baby—a cat's natural predator!—and
over the last few months, as she grew larger and larger, she
had become completely intolerable. Instead of a pleasant
cranial rub, she'd taken to gathering Garfield in her arms
and squeezing the stuffing out of him in a rush of maternal
affection. "Garfield," she'd laugh, "I'm getting almost as fat
as you!" No pat on the head was worth *this*.

He crossed the street just in case, heading toward the
house where the Constantine family lived. The two young
children, Danny and Niki, would occasionally sit on the
porch steps eating ice cream cones. One never knew when
a cone might drip, and Garfield always made a point of
strolling fetchingly across their lawn just in case. Today, no
such luck.

The Robinson home was the last house (or the first,
depending on which way you were going) at the edge of
the cul-de-sac. The word on the street was that they kept
a snake, though Garfield had never seen it. As he approached,
he thought back to the time before they moved in. Back
then, there was another family there who had not one, not
two, but *three* Japanese bobtail shorthairs that Garfield
couldn't bear, named Mama, Papa, and Baby. Precious,
mouthy little things, with stumps for tails and voices like
claws on a chalkboard. One of the happiest moments of
Garfield's life was the day the moving truck pulled up and
took them away forever.

Garfield arrived at the entrance of the cul-de-sac that was the entire world to him. *Time to inspect the edge of the universe. You never know what a new day can bring.* He settled in to watch the traffic whizzing by on the busy street, keeping one eye on an inchworm that was making its way across the sidewalk. Bored, he shot out a paw and started to toy with the poor green creature.

"Excuse me, but you're not going to eat that, are you?"

Garfield looked up to see a daddy longlegs challenging him for his catch.

"What's it to you?" Garfield inquired.

"You owe me, Garfield. You squished my girlfriend just as I was about to ask for her leg in marriage. My shattered heart will never recover."

"Get a new girlfriend," the cat suggested, batting the inchworm clear across the lawn, where it disappeared into the tall blades of grass. "It's not like we're suddenly experiencing an arachnid shortage." The spider growled and took off after the worm.

A cream-colored Siamese scampered out of the bushes and plopped himself squarely in front of Garfield.

"Morning, Garfield! Am I not the *cutest* kitten in the whole wide world?" he purred. "Could there possibly be a cuter one?"

"This is so *old*, Nermal. Do you ever tire of admiring yourself?"

"I just have a positive self-image, is all," said the little seal point, preening. "Good self-esteem is very important for developing kittens."

"Please, Nermal—you're talking to a *cat*. As a species, we are perfect at all we do, and above attempting everything else." Garfield rolled his eyes, and then narrowed them.

"Just how old are you, anyway? How come you're still a kitten?"

"Perpetual frisky youth is part of my personal charm," Nermal replied proudly. "Garfield, look! The milk truck!"

"I know, Nermal. The milk truck comes *every* day, *duh*."

"Yeah, but maybe not today. Maybe it's changing routes. Maybe this is the last we'll ever see of it! C'mon," urged Nermal. "It's just across the street. Let's go get it!" Nermal butted his cute little black-tipped ears into Garfield's behind, trying to prod him toward the crosswalk.

Garfield sat rigid. Nermal's head was no match for way too many pounds of kitty resolve.

"*No.*"

"But, Garfield . . ."

"But nothing, Nermal. I don't leave the cul-de-sac for anything. I'm safe here. Out there? A hornet's nest of trouble, I tell you. I've watched the news on TV and, despite its liberal bias, I can tell you one thing: BAD THINGS HAPPEN OUT THERE."

"But, Garfield, *milk*! Sweet, creamy, beautiful *milk*! Maybe even some half-and-half today!"

"Now hear this: I can't control 'out there,' so I don't *go* 'out there.' End of story. Besides, I've found that if you wait long enough . . ."

The delivery truck rumbled and turned into the cul-de-sac.

". . . everything comes to you." Garfield concluded with a satisfied smile. Nermal stared at him, his blue eyes wide with admiration.

"Gee, Garfield, you are *so-o-o-o* smart! I hope that when I'm old I will be as smart as you are!"

"Nermal, 'old' and 'smart' are two things you are never going to be."

14

They trotted off after the truck, which stopped in front of the Arbuckle house. The two cats crept to the side of the porch and hid behind a pail, watching the milkman remove the empty bottles and replace them with four new ones brimming with fresh milk.

"Was that a drip, Garfield?" Nermal whispered excitedly. "Did he spill some on the porch? I call it! I call the drip!"

"Those who are so easily satisfied, Nermal, *are* what they call. The drip is all yours. Right after you hop in the pail."

"Why do *I* always have to be the one in the pail?" whined Nermal.

Garfield studied the kitten coolly for a moment. "Nermal, have you ever wished you could fly?"

"No, not really."

Garfield grabbed Nermal by the paw and gestured skyward. "Think of it, Nermal. Soaring like an eagle," Garfield said, arms flapping. "The world at your feet and the wind beneath your wings. You'll be 'Nermal of the Thermals'!"

Very little of this was getting through to Nermal.

"But what about the milk?"

"Forget the milk, Nermal. It'll just weigh you down. This is your chance to *fly*!" Garfield took a running leap and landed grinning, showcasing the bucket with the flourish of a professional game show host. "Besides, there's a drip in it for you."

Thus satisfied, Nermal did as he was told and hopped into the pail.

"Where is a drum roll when you need one?" sighed the fat orange cat.

"You want I should purr?" came a small voice from the bucket.

"Did I hear right?" said Garfield, incredulous. "Nermal, did you have an *idea*?"

"Just a small one." With that, Nermal began to purr.

Garfield smoothed back his fur and took a couple of deep breaths. *Focus, focus . . .* He stretched a paw and nonchalantly yanked on a wind chime tinkling in the breeze. Then he sauntered into position and waited at the edge of the porch. The chimes struck a potted plant that raised a string that pulled on a lever that lifted the pail that seesawed a plank that turned into a downhill run for a bottle of milk that slid down the plank and—score!—tipped perfectly into the waiting open mouth of the cul-de-sac's fattest cat.

Garfield took it all in one gulp, except for the dribbles on his whiskers.

"Got milk?" he said slyly.

"I feel so *free!*" came a voice from the bucket swinging high the sky.

From the corner of his eye Garfield caught a flash of silver emerging from the garage across the street. He sprang to attention and watched the sleek cat carefully, his heart pounding faster than his usual 220 beats per minute. Sunshine glinted off her glossy coat, surrounding her with a platinum glow. She glided elegantly along the driveway, lighter than air, on four long legs that just wouldn't quit.

"Hold that thought," Garfield said, licking his paw and grooming the last of the milk from his whiskers. "The day just got more interesting."

Four kitty eyes followed her approach. *Now,* that's *the cutest cat in the whole wide world,* Garfield thought to himself. *Those ears, so soft and perky. Those whiskers—*

like butterfly wings. The luminous way the sunshine glows like gold in her eyes. And that tail . . .

"Garfield," chirped Nermal. "Is it true that Arlene is a genuine Russian blue, descended from cats that lived with Czar Nicholas II? I heard that on the fence one night. Do you think Arlene really is a princess? Huh?"

"Yes, Nermal, but not in that sense of the word. Look at the white spot on her chest. Notice the faint agouti striping in her coat. If Arlene is a genuine Russian blue, then I'm the Easter bunny's twin brother. "

"You are?"

"Yes, Nermal, I am." Garfield rolled his eyes and bounded for Arlene, which seesawed the plank that sent the empty milk bottle back whence it came, where it crashed into the lever, which dumped the pail upside down, landing Nermal with a thud and a bucket on his head.

"Fraternal twins?" came a muffled voice from under the basin.

Garfield settled next to Arlene and cleared his throat. *Time to turn on the inner rumble. No female is immune to the powers of the Love Chunky.*

"Morning, Arlene," he said, smiling suavely. "Looks like you've got an itch you just can't scratch. Perhaps I can be of service." He lifted his eyebrows a few times for emphasis.

"Go play in traffic," was the tart reply.

"Do you believe in love at first sight, Arlene, or do I have to walk by you again?" Garfield circled her twice and let out a high-pitched yowl.

"Forget it, Garfield."

"Oh, c'mon, Arlene," he purred, sidling closer. "I am but a simple cat. All I want is shelter, lasagna, regular naps, and *. . . to be loved.*" He looked deeply into her eyes. *Jon could learn a thing or two from ol' Sizzle Whiskers.*

"Not in my nine lives," she hissed.

"Not even one?"

"The traffic's right over there, Garfield, just outside the cul-de-sac," she said, jerking her head toward the end of the block. "Knock yourself out."

"What's gotten into you today, Arlene? What'd I do?"

"I think you know," she spat. "I waited *all night* for you by the fence Thursday, and you stood me up."

Garfield tried hard to remember the night in question. *Oh, right. I fell asleep watching that documentary about why lint matters.* "My cousin really needed that kidney, Arlene, and when the call comes, one must answer. Didn't I mention it?"

"That excuse didn't work *last* year, Garfield. Move along, *or else*."

Beyond Arlene, Garfield noticed a pair of oven mitts poke through a window and gently rest a steaming pecan pie on a windowsill to cool. He sat riveted to his spot, transfixed. Somewhere, music swelled—Barry White singing "Never Gonna Give You Up." His mouth started watering.

"Oh, baby. You smell so *good* today!" Garfield said, and sighed.

Arlene smirked. "You think I'm going to fall for a line like that? Puh-*leeze*."

Garfield licked his lips. "I worship you, my love. I *dream* of you. I am humbled and crumbled in your presence."

Arlene was completely taken by surprise. "Why, Garfield, I've never heard you be humbled by *anything* before! Maybe I've underestimated you." Her expression softened. "I didn't realize your feelings ran so deep. All this time I thought you were just another selfish tom . . ."

"Oh, *yeah,* baby. Deep. Deep dish, brown sugar. Rowrrr, and whipped cream on top!" Garfield looked like he might swoon.

"Whipped cream? Oh, Garfield! When did you learn to talk so pretty?" The soft silver of Arlene's cheeks deepened to a burnished pewter.

Garfield's body tensed as he prepared to make his move. His tail swished rapidly and he wiggled his butt. "I can't live without you for another minute," he said dreamily. "I want the pie. I need the pie. I've *got to have* the pie."

Resistance was futile. Casting caution to the wind, Arlene threw her head back and let out one loud "Aroooo!" She puckered up, ready for a feline frolic.

"And when I'm done," Garfield sang, "I'm going to lick the pan clean." He brushed past Arlene's waiting whiskers, hypnotized by the smells of burnt sugar and warm, buttery crust drifting in his direction.

Arlene's jaw dropped. "Huh?!? Where are you going?"

Garfield continued toward the pie.

Arlene shouted after him. "You are the most self-centered, egomaniacal cat in the entire world!"

"Don't hate me 'cause I'm beautiful," Garfield preened, crossing the street on tiptoe.

"Garfield, you're . . . IMPOSSIBLE!" Arlene turned on her heels and stormed off. *And to think I almost let that fat orange fool kiss me!*

. . . *Luca, you're IMPOSSIBLE!* A Doberman pinscher snoozed fretfully under an open window, dreaming that his pack leader was unhappy with him over an incident involving several pounds of delicious raw steak and something she called "company." With a whimper he awoke to see Garfield approaching his yard. *Aha! An intruder! I will protect the homestead. Pack Leader will be pleased. Very important to please Pack Leader.* Luca's whimper turned to a growl as he sprang to meet Garfield, teeth bared and ears flattened. He had but one thought: *Must! Defend! Turf!*

Garfield trotted calmly toward the canine missile. He'd mastered the arithmetic of Luca's choke chain years ago. All that was left to do was savor the delicious consistency with which Luca fell for the routine. *Dogs! How people could let a species that stupid into their homes, never mind trust them to patrol the perimeter, is beyond me.*

The gleaming blur of black and tan valiantly leapt the last six feet to meet the interloper at the property line. Garfield picked up speed and began the silent countdown: *Five, four, three—*

Luca strained at the leash not an inch from Garfield.

"Hmmm, my timing's off," mused Garfield, yawning. "I need sustenance, soon."

"You're on the wrong side of the street, fatso." Luca slitted his eyes and rumbled through slathering teeth.

"And you're on the wrong side of the evolutionary curve, Einstein, but I'm not one to keep score." Garfield casually inspected a paw. "Besides, I'm not overweight. I'm just under-tall."

"Keep cracking wise, Tubby."

"It's *Tabby*."

Luca's growling got louder. "Oh, you're going to get it one day. You're going to get it good!"

A tiny grin played at the corners of Garfield's mouth.

"Trust me, Luca, I get it good *every* day." He started padding through the yard, weaving in and out of a family of stone ducks lined up on the lawn. Luca followed closely, seething and dragging his chain behind him.

"Luca, do you have any idea how dumb you are? You're so dumb that it takes you a full minute to remember the 'wow' after the 'bow.' "

The Doberman yelped loudly.

"The real question," Garfield continued, "is how shall I dupe you *this* time?" Garfield's smile grew as he trotted past a garden gnome. "Come here often?" he purred to the statue. Luca snarled. His chain coiled around the elf as he crept forward.

"Shall I baffle you with simple math?" Garfield frolicked past a sprinkler head. Luca snapped at his tail. "Shall I distract you with something shiny?" Garfield ducked behind a lawn jockey, practically skipping by now. "Who's your landscaper, anyway? Some of this stuff has *got* to go. Though to a one they're all smarter and better-looking than you are. Really, what *was* Noah thinking when he put the likes of you on that ark?"

The Doberman pinscher could take no more. He trapped Garfield between the porch and a lawn chair and made his move. *"You'll never get the best of me!"* Luca roared. He lunged with all of his might at Garfield, who was whistling nonchalantly and contemplating a small red spider skittering across the chaise lonuge. He yawned.

GOYK! The chain snapped taut and caught Luca across the throat, just as it was designed to do. Luca's eyes bugged out of his head and his body crashed to the ground. It wasn't pretty.

"I think I just did," Garfield said smugly as he gazed past Luca's stubby tail.

The dog turned to look behind him, and his face fell when he saw what had been wrought. By following Garfield, Luca had wrapped his chain around every ugly statue dotting the turf that was his to defend. Furthermore, he was stuck. It would take him hours to untangle it all. Translated into dog years, it was all too much to think about. He sat. He stared. He whimpered.

Garfield burst into the happy dance of the Victorious One-Up. "Did I hear you right, dog breath? Did you call me 'fatso' earlier?" Spinning, shaking, and generally getting his groove on, the cat they call "The G" flashed his victim a most dazzling smile. "That's *phat*-so to you, fella." The G jittered boisterously into the big finale, his trademark Four-Pawed Split.

Luca was so busy being entirely confused by the silver cat's cradle before him (size: jumbo) that he could barely get off a growl.

"Jump back. Kiss myself."

"Okay, Nermal—you're up. You know the drill," Garfield said as he came upon the small Siamese happily rolling around on a nearby lawn. Nermal lay on his back with his bottom legs splayed in the "cat-as-rabbit" position and his front paws bent at the wrists on either side of his contented smile. His blue eyes were heavy, the sun was warm, and there was a butterfly to bat adorably every now and again.

With a sigh Nermal looked upside down into Garfield's billboard of a face as he hovered above, blocking the rays. "Why do *I* always have to be the one to pull the wagon, Garfield?" he whined.

THE MOVIE

"Do you really fancy another trip to Abu Dhabi?"

The Siamese sprang to attention.

"Nermal, have you ever wanted to run the Iditarod?"

"You did *what*?" Nermal cocked his head quizzically.

"It's a race, up in Alaska. World-famous, very presti-gious. So far, open to dogs only. Think of it. The first cat ever to run the Iditarod. You'd make kitty history. You could get interviewed on television."

"I'm *perfect* for television" said Nermal, warming to the prospect. "Looks sell, and I'm the cutest kitten in the whole wide world."

"You can't train too early or too much for such a difficult race, Nermal. Go get the wagon. Mush."

A short while later, Garfield marched down the street, nose in the air and tail held high, to the roar of the crowd and the tune of Wagner's "Ride of the Valkyries" playing in his head. Nermal followed, stumbling to keep up, for be-tween his teeth was a shoelace that was attached to a roller skate, atop which sat one still-warm pecan pie. Fading be-hind them were the pathetic whimpers of the world's most unhappy dog.

"I love the smell of pecan in the morning," purred Gar-field, inhaling deeply. "Smells like . . . *victory*."

Chapter Three

Garfield was spread out on the dark green easy chair, licking crumbs from his whiskers. He propped his hind legs on the empty pie plate and pawed the remote control.

Oh, wise and magnificent picture box. Let me bask in the aura of your glory. Fill me with your wisdom. I am your humble vessel, except for the part of me holding the pie right now. He patted his stomach, which in his particular shade of fur looked remarkably like a basketball. Garfield shifted in his favorite chair until his belly no longer obstructed his view of the television.

Let's see what's happening on the Mello in the Morning *show today.*

A tall blond woman in a short black skirt strutted across the stage and introduced the star with a smile and a swish of her hand. "Ladies and gentlemen, dogs and cats (we know you're out there!), say hello to your host, Christopher Mello!" A large, bald black man in a suit and tie entered from between two curtains, arms outstretched in a wide welcome.

"Hello, everybody! Are you 'mello' this morning? I sure hope so, because we have a big show for you, a really big show. Today we'll hear from an expert on how to make your own no-sew window curtains, the trend that's sweeping the state. Next we'll preview the new production of *I Love You, You're Perfect, Now Fix Me a Sandwich Already*, debuting at the Variety Arts Music Fair next week. But first, let's have a big hand for one of our favorite 'mello' regulars, Happy Chapman!"

"Hey, folks! Do you love your cat?" An imposing yet friendly middle-aged man bounded onscreen and addressed Garfield from inside the television. Despite broadcasting from the nearby city, he was wearing a safari suit.

Who doesn't *love their cat?* Garfield shot back

"If you love your cat as much as I do, you'll only feed it Kibbly Kat Food . . ."

Ah, Kibbly. Good stuff. A tad on the dry side, and it will never compete with lasagna, but it's an important part of my well-rounded—he rubbed his fat tummy—*diet.*

"Isn't that right, Persnikitty? Persnikitty?? Where *is* that danged cat?" chortled Happy.

Here comes my favorite part. Some genius at the studio figured out that this could get old fast, so they keep things fresh by putting the cat in a different outfit every time. Then, at the end of the season, the audience votes, and Persnikitty gets his picture taken in the winning ensemble for the next print run of the Kibbly Kat food box. This idea must have kept the marketing boys up all night. Garfield leaned forward, transfixed by the flickering screen. *Persnikitty is one of those cats who looks good no matter what he puts on, what with that basic black and white coloring. What* will *he be wearing this time?*

GARFIELD

Right on cue, the cat that made Kibbly famous scampered into the picture, outfitted in a tweed vest and a cunning fedora hat. He buried his face in the food bowl as Happy stroked and gazed upon him lovingly.

If Jon ever tried anything like that while I was eating, I would have to take his hand off.

Garfield heard the sound of tires on the driveway, but there was no point in exerting himself just yet. It would be inefficient. He continued to watch Persnikitty suck down the bowl of Kibbly crunchy goodness.

That cat's face is everywhere. On TV, in books, on T-shirts, everything. Who would want that kind of exposure?

At the sound of the key in the lock, Garfield's ears flickered. *Okay, now it's time to show Jon how mad I am that he left the house. Shall I shed on his toothbrush? Do the thousand-sheet toilet paper pull? Unless . . . Yes!* There it was, the distinctive, delicate rustle of that source of all good things, the grocery bag. Jon came through the door.

All is forgiven. Welcome home.

"Garfield, get out of my chair," Jon said, taking in the pie plate and the crumbs with a *What now?* expression on his face.

It's my chair, and you just get to sit in it. Besides, I clash with that burgundy velvet sofa. Still, I need to see what you've brought home from the market, so your wish is granted. Garfield leapt lightly to the floor and trotted into the kitchen.

"Good boy!" Jon said, beaming, and placed the bags carefully on the kitchen counter. He hummed to himself as he crossed the room to put the new cheese in the refrigerator.

THE MOVIE

Garfield saw his opening, and he went for it. In a burst of energy deployed exclusively in culinary matters, he quietly jumped his way to the counter and sniffed around the bags. He sat up on his haunches and stretched to get a better look, then rose on his hind legs to stick his head completely into the bag.

Crash! Four boxes of Papa Luigi's frozen lasagna tumbled to the floor, with Garfield in hot pursuit. As he patted one with his paw, he could hear Happy Chapman's signature sign-off coming from the television in the next room. "And remember . . . be happy!"

I'm happy when I'm with you, *you delicate mélange of tomato paste, ricotta cheese, ground meat, and pasta,* Garfield crooned lovingly to the boxes, which were sweating from either fear or condensation.

Jon knew the look on his cat's face all too well. "Don't even *think* about it, Garfield," he said, staring the cat down through the half-closed eyes of one weary from the battle. "That's *my* food." With that, Jon shooed Garfield away from the mess on the floor and went back out to the car to fetch the rest of the bags.

Garfield sat in the kitchen doorway, nonplussed. He glanced at the television, where Persnikitty was getting a mighty hug from a devoted Happy. "Nothing's too good for my little friend," said the man in the pith helmet.

I don't get "Nothing's too good for my little friend." Oh, no. I get "Don't even THINK about it." Why can't Jon be more like Happy Chapman? I'll bet Happy's *a hit with the ladies.*

Garfield sat and stewed and stared at the lasagna, while from the television, Happy Chapman and Christopher

Mello signed off and blew big wet kisses at the viewing public.

A moment later, in a tall, pointy building in the big city, a stage manager said, "And we're out." The smile instantly disappeared from Happy's face as the camera went to black. This was followed by the sort of hundred-mile-per-hour sneeze that makes everybody duck for cover and think, *Ewwwww!*

"Get this thing away from me, Wendell," spat Happy, tossing Persnikitty to his assistant. "Freakin' allergies. Where the devil is my allergy medicine?"

Wendell caught the frazzled, slightly damp feline and cradled him in one arm as he rooted through his pockets to find the medication. Happy continued to sneeze, with each eruption more spectacular than the last. Wendell offered his boss a tissue, which was refused.

They walked through the studio as Happy sucked down the pill. "We hear anything back from the network yet?"

"They're looking for a dog act on *Good Day, New York*," Wendell said.

"A *dog* act? Well, isn't *that* the story of my life! They want a dog act and I'm stuck with this worthless cat."

Persnikitty squirmed in Wendell's arms and hissed at Happy.

"I thought the segment went quite well. The fedora was a nice touch."

"Of course it went well, you toad," Happy sneered. "The fifty housewives who saw it *loved* it!" He smacked Wendell upside the head for emphasis. Then he sneezed again.

Wendell blotted his face with the tissue as they neared a

THE MOVIE

TV monitor broadcasting international news. The anchor looked an awful lot like Happy, except that he wore a three-thousand-dollar double-breasted English-cut suit instead of safari gear and a goofy hat.

"The joint commission on world famine begins tomorrow. For now, this is Walter J. Chapman reporting live from The Hague . . ."

"Hey, isn't that your brother?" asked Wendell. "You guys resemble each other. What's the 'J' stand for?"

" 'J' as in *jerk*!" said Happy, who at the moment really wasn't. " '*Live from The Hague,*' " he mocked. "Please. What a know-it-all. People always said *I* was the handsome one. *I* was the smart one. I was BORN FIRST!" *Ah-choo!* "Yet here *he* is, 'reporting live from The Hague,' while I'm stuck working with this sack of dander on some dead-end regional morning show!"

The rumble grew louder in Persnikitty's throat, and Happy sneezed once more.

Back at the Arbuckle home, Jon entered the house with the rest of the grocery bags, and couldn't believe his eyes. Or maybe he could, for there was Garfield licking his paw and rubbing his face with it, surrounded by empty cartons.

"Garfield! You ate *all four* boxes of lasagna?!?" Jon was bright red with anger. "How on earth did you do that? I was gone for only a second!"

It's not my fault, Jon. I needed something to wash down the pie. Garfield pawed the picture of Papa Luigi on the nearest box. *Besides, he started it.*

Jon bent over to clean up the mess, shaking his head. "What am I going to *do* with you?"

GARFIELD

Love me. Feed me. Never leave me.

"C'mon," Jon sighed, resignation tainting his voice. "Let's go for a ride to some place you really love that always leaves you feeling refreshed and pampered."

The Pasta Palace?

Jon scooped his beloved cat up into his arms, grabbed the keys, and walked out the door.

Garfield grew reflective. *Most cats really hate going for a ride in the car. It makes them nervous. They usually end up shredding the upholstery or clinging to the top of the driver's head. Occasionally, blood is drawn. Me, I'm not like the other cats. I'm a great little traveler.*

Jon opened the passenger door and placed Garfield in his own special car seat. He strapped him in securely, swung the door shut, and walked around to the driver's side.

The only time I ever leave my cul-de-sac is when we go on vacation, or Jon takes me to the vet. We've been going to the vet a lot recently, and it has nothing to do with me. Jon wants to go for his own reason.

Ever careful, the man with his own reason backed the car out of the driveway and drove slowly down the block. They passed Nermal and Arlene sunning themselves on the walk in front of the Constantine house. Danny and Niki were throwing a ball back and forth on the front lawn.

Nermal looked up. "Hey, Arlene. Where do you think Garfield is going?"

"I don't know, Nermal," she said, still smarting from their earlier encounter. "But wherever it is, I hope it's a one-way ticket." She sniffed and turned her back to the car, which continued toward the main road.

Garfield looked out the window at the beautiful sight of

Luca, still tangled, getting yelled at by his pack leader. "And furthermore," she screamed, "you'll get no dinner tonight because you're so full of PECAN PIE!"

Days just don't get better than this.

"Hey, Luca!" Garfield called to the dog. "What do you call ten Dobermans at the bottom of the ocean?"

Luca looked up and whined.

"A good beginning!" roared Garfield as they rolled past.

The car reached the end of the cul-de-sac and Jon day-dreamed aloud as he waited for the traffic light to change.

"I hope Liz isn't too busy to see us today, Garfield. We don't actually have an appointment. I thought it might be fun to pop in and surprise her."

Listen to me, Jon. You're going about this all wrong. Haven't you learned by now the value of playing hard-to-get with the ladies? If you slobber all over her like some big, stupid dog, it's just going to be you and me every Saturday night for the rest of your life. I'm not sure I'm up to that sort of responsibility.

"Maybe the time is right to ask her out on a date. I don't want to appear too pushy. We've only known each other since 1985."

Get with the century, Jon. Behold the Round Mound of Romance the next night I'm out aroooing Arlene. Learn from the Thrillmeister. Oh, wait. You're barely awake by nine-thirty or ten. Never mind.

Jon's pupils swelled and a goofy smile began to take shape. "Ahhh, Liz. Wonderful Liz, beautiful Liz, *irrepressible* Liz!" His foot slipped and the car lurched forward. Jon slammed on the brakes, tossing Garfield in his kitty seat. "Sorry, Garfield! She makes me forget where I am! Are you okay over there?"

GARFIELD

Where did you get your license, pal, the gumball machine?

The light changed to green and Jon cautiously turned the car out of the cul-de-sac. Through the window, Garfield saw his silvery muse on the walk, her back to him, her nose high in the air, and her tail twitching furiously.

Chapter Four

Jon pushed open the heavy glass door on which ELIZA-BETH WILSON, DVM was stenciled in bold blue letters. Garfield strode in first, scanning the waiting room for alien life forms. The chairs were empty except for a bald, middle-aged man sitting with a hamster on his lap.

Garfield went over to investigate as Jon approached the receptionist.

Mmmmm, hamster.

The pile of spotted fur quivered in the man's lap, nose twitching. First he blinked one eye, and then the other, but never both at the same time, because hamsters can't do that.

"Easy, Hansel," said the man. "It's just a friendly old kitty."

Garfield propped his front paws on the man's knee and drew himself up to get a better view.

"See how nice he is?" He extended a hand and scratched Garfield under his chin.

Do you know how I like hamsters?

Garfield stretched his neck to luxuriate in the attention and whispered right into Hansel's ear.

Barbecued.

The hamster squeaked uncontrollably and scrabbled up

his owner's thigh, digging his claws in until there were tears streaming down the bald man's face.

"Garfield!" Jon said sharply. "Leave that poor creature alone!" Garfield crossed the floor and started chewing on a silk plant. Jon turned back to the woman sitting behind the desk.

"As I was saying, we don't actually *have* an appointment today, and no, it's not exactly an emergency, but if Liz—er, if Dr. Wilson has some time in her schedule, I'd really appreciate it if she would just take a quick look. At Garfield, I mean. He doesn't seem quite himself to me. Also, he could use a flea dip."

The receptionist looked over her half-moon glasses at Garfield, who playfully chased a rubber band around the floor. He leapt, slammed his two front paws down onto the cunning prey, stuck his butt up in the air, thrashed his head back and forth a few times, and howled.

"I see what you mean," she said dryly. "I've never seen Garfield move that much for any reason at all. I'm sure the doctor will be able to squeeze him in after Hansel."

Jon walked to the waiting area and sat. He looked over the magazines stacked neatly on the table beside him. "Let's see—*Mushing*, *Paint Horse Journal*, *Miniature Donkey Talk*, *Reptile and Amphibian Hobbyist*, *Coonhound Bloodlines* . . . ah, here we go. *I Love Cats!*" He slid the magazine from the pile and started to flip through the pages.

He read aloud from the table of contents. " 'Your Cat: Fat or Fit?' " Jon glanced over at Garfield, who was lying on his back with his paws up in the air. He couldn't see Garfield's face because his stomach was in the way.

With a heavy sigh he turned to the article. " 'The average weight of a healthy adult cat ranges from eight to eighteen pounds (3.5 to 8 kg), depending on the breed and the size of the cat's frame,' " he read. " 'Fortunately, most cats have a natural tendency to stop eating when full, and will devote a portion of their day to the playful activity necessary to keep their caloric intake in healthy balance.' " Jon glanced up at Garfield, who had fallen asleep.

The receptionist beckoned to the bald man. "The doctor will see Hansel now. Won't you please step this way?"

As the man and his hamster disappeared through the Dutch door, Garfield turned over in his sleep and gave a little snort.

Jon shook his head and put the magazine back on the table. He was too nervous to concentrate on reading, anyway. *Soon it will be our turn,* he thought, his palms beginning to sweat just a little. He pictured Liz in her crisp white lab coat, a stethoscope slung fetchingly around a neck that could put a swan to shame. Add to that the brilliant smile, raindrops for eyes, and a genuine concern for her patients, and Jon Arbuckle, Successful Cartoonist, was a wobbly mess of junior-high jitters.

Maybe I should practice, he thought. He looked around. He had the waiting area all to himself, since the receptionist had taken Hansel back to the examination room. He spotted a decorative mirror on the wall, next to a doggie dental hygiene poster. Jon cleared his throat, upon which Garfield opened one eye.

"Why, good morning, Liz!" he said, addressing his reflection. "Aren't *you* as beautiful as a country farm in the summertime, only you don't smell as bad!"

Garfield sat up and cocked his head.

"No, no—that's not it," thought Jon out loud.

No kidding, Romeo. Try again.

"How about 'Your eyes shine like oil slicks on a dew-sprinkled country road'?"

Garfield sighed heavily and his fur stuck out on end.

Jon leaned into the mirror, fluttered his eyebrows, and crooned. "You know, if we cut off your arms, you'd look just like the Venus de Milo!"

Garfield started to howl and writhe on the floor.

"Goodness, Garfield, are you okay?"

Both man and cat froze at the sound of a familiar, melodious voice. There stood Liz Wilson, DVM, with a look of concern stretched across her perfect complexion.

Jon tried to speak but produced no actual words. Liz smiled.

"Let's take you into the back and have a look at you."

She means me, Lothario. Garfield hopped up and walked in and out of Liz's legs, rubbing them affectionately and meowing as he looked up at her face. She scooped him into her arms and nuzzled his soft cheeks. Garfield licked her nose. They turned toward the back rooms.

Jon contemplated leaving town and followed them in silence.

"There's nothing wrong with Garfield, Jon. He's just a lazy, happy, fat cat," said Liz as she felt up and down his considerable torso.

I want a second opinion. Garfield extended a paw to bat playfully at the pendant swinging from her neck, careful to keep his claws retracted. She tickled his belly and laughed. "What a sweetie you are, Garfield."

The ol' feline charm never fails . . .

Jon stood by, gaga and tongue-tied.

. . . unlike the ol' Arbuckle charm. Watch, Jon. Learn at

the feet of Catsanova. He closed his eyes (but not quite all the way), snuggled a rusty cheek against her hand, and purred loudly. Liz nuzzled Garfield's face.

Jon finally found his voice. "I worry about him."

"I know you do. You care about him more than any owner I've ever seen," Liz said gently.

Let's drop the "third kitty invisible" tense, shall we? "Him" has a name. What is this, an HMO?

Liz stroked the vast expanse of soft ginger fur. "Why don't we send Garfield back for his dip? I'd like a word with you in private."

There's nothing you can say to Jon that can't be said in front of me.

At the words *in private,* Jon's heart pounded almost clear out of his chest. As Liz went to get an assistant, two love-struck eyes followed her. "She is *so* beautiful," he breathed.

You've had a crush on her since high school. Have at it already, Jon. Then she can dump you and I can get on with my life.

"I've *got* to ask her out," he said, petting his cat absent-mindedly. "Wish me luck, Garfield."

If you insist. Garfield leapt up and proceeded to dance across the examination table. *You the man! Fettuccine, baby! Like butter! Be the boss! Preach to her!* He grabbed Jon by the shirt buttons and pulled until they were eye to eye. *It's all YOU, Bubba!*

Jon rolled his eyes and said icily, "Finished yet?"

The assistant entered the room, picked up Garfield, and carried him out.

Dead man walking.

They headed down the hall to the dip room.

GARFIELD

I'll start with a little deep tissue massage, then maybe a seaweed wrap. Some shiatsu, perhaps, and a steam to open up my chest. Do you have any sashimi to go with that? A magazine? Next, a leisurely belly rub, then we can finish up with a nice loofah. Thanks.

The nurse plopped Garfield in a basin and left the room. A technician began splashing him, working the dip into his fur with gloved fingers. Two salmon ears flattened and Garfield's tail began to thrash, launching a tsunami in the sink and soaking the veterinary assistant.

I will, without remorse or hesitation, make you wish you'd called in sick today if you don't put an end to this nonsense immediately. Garfield jumped out of the basin and onto the counter. With one mighty shake of his enormous soggy body, he managed to knock over every jar, vial, and box within five feet. This cheered him right up.

Jon floated after Liz as she walked down the hall to her office. She sat behind the desk and started rummaging around, looking for something. Jon took a seat across from her.

"Jon, I've got something important to ask you." Her expression grew serious. "Something I wouldn't *think* of asking most of the guys that come in here."

Could he believe his ears? Jon's heart began to pound. He prayed Liz couldn't hear it. "Wait. No. I think I know where this is going," he stammered, the excitement rising in his voice.

"You do?" Her glistening raindrop eyes widened.

"I do, Liz," he said, looking at her intently. "I've wanted to ask you the same thing for a very long time . . ."

Liz was confused. "You *have*?"

THE MOVIE

Emboldened by her response, Jon propped his elbows on the desk and rested his chin in his hands, searching her face. "Yeah. You see, I've done pretty well for myself . . . or it looks that way . . . but something's always been missing. Something that's been right in front of me since the tenth grade." He batted his lashes ever so slightly.

Liz looked at him quizzically. "Jon, is there something in your eye? And are we talking about the same thing?"

"Absolutely!" he exclaimed, silently ordering his eyelids to a halt. "I've never been more sure of anything in my entire life. I'm ready, Liz, ready to take a chance. I'm ready for the commitment. I'm ready for . . ."

At that moment, a small, goofy-looking dog scooted out from behind the desk. He scrambled onto Jon's lap and licked his face, slobbering all the way.

". . . a *dog*??"

Liz laughed. "It looks like he likes you!"

Indeed it was a dog, a dinky tan mutt tipped with brown on his paws, tail, and floppy ears. The tail went *thump, thump, thump* as he continued to lick Jon's face all over. He had an unusually large tongue for one so small.

"Frisky little fella," Jon giggled, unable to resist such a warm welcome from, well, *anyone*.

Liz looked in the folder she'd found and her voice grew somber. "His name is Odie, and he didn't have it very good before he came here. He's not going to make it if he has to live his life in a cage. He needs to be loved."

"Don't we all . . ." Jon muttered under his breath.

Liz didn't hear him. "And I think you're just the man for the job. So, do me a favor. Take him home with you."

"Huh?!?" Jon smiled squeamishly and squirmed in his chair. The dog enjoyed the ride. "Home? Him? Me?"

Liz looked into his eyes and straight through to his soul. She reached across the desk and touched Jon gently on the arm. "Yes, him. You."

Jon melted instantly, although the puddle that formed in his lap came from the steady supply of drool provided by the dog. Odie let out a happy yelp and licked Jon under his chin. Suddenly, there was going to be a new dog in the cul-de-sac.

Back in the grooming area, the technician was using a blow dryer to put the finishing touch on Garfield's tiger-striped coat. The cat caught himself in a mirror and admired his fluffed-out pompadour. He grabbed an imaginary microphone and struck a pose. *Thankyouverahmuch. Elvis is ready to leave the building.*

And that's enough of that. Garfield shook himself violently until his fur returned to its customary state of matted knots. He looked around the room, which was filled with pets of all kinds in cages, waiting for the treatments they had come for.

"Yo! Fat cat! Settle an argument for us," meowed a sleek Cornish rex. He jerked his nose toward a poster hanging on the wall. It read KIBBLY KAT PET FOOD and featured a picture of a smiling Happy Chapman surrounded by a gaggle of animals. From a speech bubble came Happy's famous—if not overly simplistic—slogan, "BE HAPPY!"

Garfield looked at the poster.

"Who makes the better chow," asked the rex, "Kibbly or Yummy Cat?"

Garfield didn't miss a beat. "Neither, you moron. The correct answer is 'Papa Luigi.' "

The animals looked at each other, puzzled.

"Well, I'd love to stay and chat, boys, but I've got to get back to Jon. He can't stand it when I leave him for too long. Yep, I've got him right where I want him," he bragged. "We both love the same thing . . . *me*. Besides, he's been alone too long with the vet. I expect that by now a little damage control will be in order. *Ciao*."

The technician returned Garfield to Jon, who was standing in the waiting room with Liz. The cat leapt from his arms and padded toward the exit. The humans followed behind at a respectful ten paces.

"Jon, look. You really don't have to do this if you don't want to," said Liz.

"It's okay," he replied. "Some part of me has always wondered what it would be like to have a pet that actually wants to play with you."

Liz laughed. "You really are a good friend. And I want you to know that I'll be here to help make the transition go smoothly. We could all go out together, you know, to the park. To dog shows. Stuff like that."

Jon stopped dead in his tracks. "Wait a minute. You're asking *me* out?" His heart was thudding a mile a minute.

Liz smiled knowingly, said nothing, and headed back into her office. Jon's spirits soared.

Jon was still hyperventilating near the entrance when Garfield reached the car. Four paws skidded to a halt, and one kitty jaw hit the pavement. *No! It couldn't be! It IS NOT POSSIBLE.*

There was Odie, sitting up front in Garfield's special seat and drooling cheerfully on the armrest. Garfield stared, frozen, in utter disbelief. He walked around the car and then looked again. The dog was still there, grinning at

Garfield through the glass window. Jon ambled up and keyed the lock.

Oh, Jonny-boy. I think it's time you got a car alarm. It seems a mongrel mutt has broken into your car.

Jon opened the door and looked down at his cat. "Garfield, this is Odie. He's coming home with us."

Garfield slapped himself on the forehead. *Whoa! You went in there to get a date and came out with a DOG? No, no, no. That's bad, even for you.* He waggled his finger at Jon. *We are NOT bringing a dog home with us. Toss this crotch-sniffer back on the pile and let's get going.* He sat himself squarely on the pavement, ears back, and threatened his master with his eyes.

Jon picked up Garfield and placed him gently in the backseat.

Hey! Garfield had never even seen the backseat before, much less ridden there. This was adding insult to injury. Jon slammed the door shut and headed around to the driver's side. With a blank expression on his face, Odie turned to look at the seething ottoman of orange fur, whose eyes were boring into the dog from behind.

What are you looking at, tick boy? Garfield was practically hissing. This whizzed past Odie completely. He panted a few times and made himself comfortable in Garfield's seat as Jon steered the car out of the parking lot. He hung his head out the window, hung his tongue out of his head, and took in the local sights as they sped by.

Jon whistled to himself as he pulled up to the local pet supply store. Garfield was still fuming in the backseat. Odie was still drooling in the front.

This is how Jon thinks he's going to make this up to

me? Buying me off with some cheap rubber squeaky toy? I THINK NOT.

"Odie, we need to get you some things." Jon got out of the car and stuck his head back inside. "Most importantly, we've got to buy you some food. Garfield's not really the type to share, are you, Garfield?" A deep rumble sounded from the back.

Jon rolled the rear window down an inch, loosened the straps on the special seat, and backed out of the car. "Come on, Odie. Here, boy!"

Odie sat there, sniffing the dashboard.

"Odie, come on! Let's go shopping!" Jon laughed. "Maybe you haven't really learned your name yet. Well, we'll work on that." He motioned wildly to the dog, who noticed a moth flying by just outside the car and jumped after it. Jon closed the door and the pair trotted across the parking lot.

Garfield vaulted to the front seat, scrambled up the dashboard, and plastered himself to the windshield with his paws splayed. He pressed his nose against the glass and watched them recede into the distance, taking his perfect happiness with them.

Inside the store, Jon placed Odie in the shopping cart and headed for the dog section. "Wow, Odie—I've never been down *these* aisles before. It's a whole new world! Just like you're going to be, I'll bet." He scratched Odie affectionately behind the ears. "There were dogs back on the farm where I grew up, but they weren't really mine. I was more of a cat and pig person. The dogs always loved my brother Doc Boy best." Odie clambered up the cart and licked Jon's face noisily. "But not you, Odie," Jon said in baby talk. "Doc Boy is not going to be *your* favorite-wavorite, is he?"

Odie's head swiveled enthusiastically as he absorbed the colorful marvels all around him. Every time he turned to take in some new wonder, he splashed a little drool on Jon's hands.

"Just wait until you get to know Garfield." Jon beamed, wiping his fingers on his pants. "You're going to love him. I know he's a little gruff at first, and he can be moody sometimes. A more cynical cat you'll probably never meet. And it's generally a good idea to let him have his way—or else—but really, after you spend some time with him, you'll love him just as much as I do. He's really easy to get along with once you learn to worship him properly."

Odie let out a merry bark and panted with joy.

Jon laughed. "Happy little fellow, aren't you? Good! We're going to get along just fine. Look, here are the collars. Which one do you like best? Show me." Odie drooled over all of them, regardless of color or style. He looked at Jon with an expression of pure devotion.

"All *righty*, then! We'll just take this one," Jon said, selecting the driest collar. He sneaked glances to see if anyone had noticed his dog saturating the merchandise. "All clear. Let's move on, shall we?" They wandered the aisles until the basket was brimming with all of the items on their list, not to mention the dog that inspired their purchase.

Jon pushed the cart toward the checkout. They passed a wall of cat toys. Jon stopped to study them. "I really must get something for Garfield. He's been my constant companion for more years than I can count. We've had so many wonderful times together, Odie. Fishing trips, pepper-eating contests, waiting up for Santa . . . There couldn't possibly be a better friend on this earth than my Garfield. Or should

I say, '*our* Garfield' now!" Jon selected a squeaky rubber hamburger and showed it to Odie. "He doesn't have this one yet. Do you think he'll like it? He's nuts for the real thing." Odie licked the bun, and Jon got on line to pay for their purchases.

Garfield watched Jon and Odie enter the pet store. As the door slid closed behind them, he fell from the windshield and let out a plaintive howl. In his mind he saw Odie taking his place in the shopping basket, and it was more than he could bear. He howled once more, louder this time.

"*Psssst.* Cat. What's your damage?"

Garfield turned to see an Irish setter, well, *setting* in the SUV parked next to Jon's modest little car. Her nose poked out from the small open space her owner had left at the top of the window.

"You'd never understand," sniffed Garfield. "You're a dog. Worse, you're an Irish setter. Such a *big* dog, with such a tiny little brain. They don't come any dumber than you." He thought of Odie, stealing Jon's heart in aisle three. "Except maybe . . ."

"There, there," said the setter. "You're only talking this way because you're very upset about something."

"You don't know me very well, do you?"

The kind red hound overlooked this last remark. "Let me guess. Your pack leader has just brought home a new pet and you're worried about losing your place in the family. How am I doing so far?"

"Pack leader? *I* wear the pants in this household."

"No doubt." The setter laughed softly to herself. "Listen, I've been there. From the day they brought me home from

45

the breeder, they only had eyes for me. It was always 'Scarlet this,' and 'Scarlet that,' and 'Isn't Scarlet the sweetest, most beautiful dog you've ever seen?' Then one Christmas, in walks the pack leader with a kitten under his arm. For the rest of that winter these people forgot to feed or walk me unless I reminded them. Suddenly, it was all *'Fluffy* this,' and *'Fluffy* that,' and 'Isn't *Fluffy* the sweetest, most beautiful kitty you've ever seen?' I became *canine non grata* around there."

Garfield swallowed hard. *Will Jon forget to feed me?? Not that! ANYTHING but that!*

"But after a while the novelty wore off, and by the time Easter rolled around, things improved," Scarlet continued. "Fluffy got bigger and wasn't nearly as cute anymore, and it turns out she has a mean streak a mile wide and almost as deep. Now the children are terrified of her." Scarlet smiled triumphantly. "And they hadn't *really* forgotten how wonderful I am. They were just distracted by 'the new toy' for a little while. Now I'm back on top where I belong. Yup, I've got that annoying little Fluffy exactly where I want her."

Garfield looked at Scarlet through the window, considering her story. *Maybe Jon will get tired of Odie and things will go back to the way they were back when life was still good, about half an hour ago. The only problem is, Odie's not snotty like Fluffy is. Drooly, maybe, but not snotty.*

Scarlet's owner returned to the car, got in, and turned the key in the ignition. *Remember what I'm telling you, cat. Things look bleak at the moment, but they'll work out, you'll see.* The SUV backed out and pulled away.

THE MOVIE

Garfield spied Jon and Odie emerging from the pet store. Jon's arms were loaded with packages, and Odie jumped and danced playfully at his heels. Jon laughed and said, "Well, aren't *you* the sweetest, cutest thing!"

If Garfield had taken any comfort from Scarlet's story, all his hopes now came a-tumbling down.

Chapter Five

Jon steered the car into the driveway and rolled to a stop. He and Odie climbed out of the front seat. Garfield continued to sulk in the back.

"C'mon, Garfield. We're home."

"We." HA! I remember when "we" was just thee and me. Garfield took his time getting out of the car. Jon was too busy getting bags from the trunk to notice.

Brimming with energy, Odie bounced all over his new yard, sniffing this, nudging that, and rolling around in the lush green grass. He raised a leg at one of the boulders flanking the path.

Garfield took all of this in with great annoyance. *Don't even* think *about marking my rock, dog breath, or this will be your last day on earth.* Odie proceeded to prove he hadn't heard a word of it, and Garfield hissed loudly.

Odie ran to Jon and pulled playfully at the bags dangling from his arms. Jon smooshed Odie on the head. "You're one frisky little fella, aren't you, Odie?" Odie slobbered with pleasure and followed Jon to the front door. Garfield watched in horror from his spot on the concrete. Nermal and Arlene wandered over from across the street and sat down.

THE MOVIE

"Garfield, Jon brought a dog home," said Nermal, looking a bit confused.

"I'm aware of this, Nermal."

"Why would he do a thing like that?"

Garfield flattened his ears and turned toward him with a murderous look, which flew right past the small buff-colored Siamese. "I don't *know*, Nermal."

Nermal shook his adorable but mostly empty head. "I mean, it just seems like a weird thing to do, you know? Bringing a dog into a house that already has a cat?"

Garfield exploded. "CAN WE DROP IT???" Nermal and Arlene jumped about three feet straight up, all rigid and spiky. Garfield collected himself and nonchalantly groomed his shoulder. "I mean, it's no big, fat, hairy deal. Just a gnat on the windshield of my existence. A dimwitted, smelly, goofy gnat that I will deal with appropriately, in due time."

Wobbling from the weight of his purchases, Jon looked back from the porch and called to Garfield.

"As you can see, folks, I'm still Jon's favorite," he said smugly. He turned on his heels, raised his head high, and strutted toward the house. Odie ran in ahead of Jon, who stepped inside and absentmindedly slammed the door behind him just as Garfield reached it.

Nermal and Arlene exchanged knowing looks.

"Ha ha ha!" Garfield roared, laughing perhaps a bit too hard. "I guess this makes up for the 'catnip in the breakfast cereal' gag! What a masterpiece! You should have been there. Even better than the time I sent a pair of Jon's bunny slippers for a spin in the blender!" He tipped his paw in farewell and squeezed through the kitty door, but the manufacturer had never considered a cat the size of Orson Welles.

Wiggling through took a while, tarnishing what might other-wise have been a clean getaway.

The kitty door turned out to be a portal to Garfield's worst nightmare.

Inside, the brave kitty's game face crashed to the floor. Odie was leaning up against Jon, wagging his tail and fog-ging up the glass coffee table. Jon was introducing Odie to his new home.

"This is the living room, Odie. LI-VING ROOM." Jon spoke slowly and loudly, as if his listener couldn't under-stand English, which, in fact, he couldn't.

Jon, what are you doing? It's not staying.

Odie got up on his hind legs and started to hop around in circles. Jon laughed and grabbed a paw. "You want to dance with me? OK, let's Lindy!" Jon spun Odie around and smushed his ears.

This is so pathetic.

Odie had scampered into the kitchen and was investigat-ing the trash. He returned to the LI-VING ROOM carrying an empty Papa Luigi lasagna box between his teeth.

Garfield crouched on the floor, threw back his ears, and thrashed his tail. *Oh, no you don't. Forget about Papa Luigi, pal. You never met him, you never heard of him, you don't know nuthin', capisce?*

Jon delighted in watching Odie skitter around the house. "You're curious about everything, aren't you, boy?" Jon laughed. "Go ahead, give the whole place a good, long sniff!"

As far as cats are concerned, Jon, curiosity never killed anything, except maybe a dull afternoon. I'm not mak-ing any promises about the dog.

Odie coasted on his butt across the polished wood floor and crashed into a wall.

"This is Sushi, our goldfish," Jon said, pointing to the coffee table. Odie trotted over and started to drink from the fishbowl. "No, Odie! Don't do that!" Jon cried, though he couldn't help but laugh. "I can see you have a mind of your own."

He's welcome to it. Who else would want it?

"I have some things to take care of upstairs. I'll leave you guys to get acquainted. Garfield can finish giving you the tour," Jon said, smiling. Odie yipped with joy and scrambled at top speed straight for Garfield, tumbling over the frozen cat and slamming into the front door. He slid to the floor. *Plop.*

Jon, can't you see? Wake up and smell the dog breath: BRAIN NOT INCLUDED! You've brought a household hazard into our previously well-balanced environment. Everything's out of kilter now. Jon! Where are you going?

Jon was climbing the stairs to the bedroom, carrying a large waterproof pillow under his arm. "Have fun, you two."

Garfield hunkered down on the Sacred Chair, tucked in his paws, and curled his tail around himself. He watched Odie as he ricocheted like a pinball from bookcase to sofa to potted plant.

This is just a bad dream. When you wake up, everything will be back to normal. Garfield squeezed his peepers shut. *One one-thousand, two one-thousand, three one-thousand . . .* He smelled the truth before he opened his eyes to see the enemy within an inch of his face. Odie planted a big, wet slurp squarely on his whiskers. The sensation gave Garfield the skeevies.

Great. Dog cooties. Tell me, do your fleas have flood insurance?

WHOMP!

With a vigorous shove, Garfield sent Odie flying across the floor. The trip ended abruptly at the hutch that held Jon's sea-monkey collection, sending a lifetime's worth of brine shrimp crashing to the floor.

I should do a practice run. Garfield cleared his throat. *"Hey, Jon! Look what the dog did!"*

Considerably cheered, Garfield walked to the coffee table to retrieve the television remote. He turned back just in time to see Odie splash-landing on the lounger. Garfield marched over with great determination.

No. NO. NO! I know you're new here, but we have to get some rules straight. This is my chair. MY chair, despite what Jon might tell you. Okay? I even SEE you raise a leg and IT'S ON!

Odie was busy sniffing the cushion in search of just the right spot and hadn't noticed Garfield at all. He plopped down comfortably and yawned.

Garfield wiped the drool from his eye. *Very well, then. I have given you fair warning.* Garfield held up a paw and—*PING!* Out shot five claws, one by one for dramatic effect, which was completely lost on poor Odie, who watched with benign fascination. After one last showy flex of the wrists, Garfield jammed a glittering claw into Odie's butt.

Odie yelped at the top of his lungs and flipped head over ears off the easy chair, landing with a *thwonk!* on the other side of the television. He licked and soothed the wound, at last putting some of that drool to good use, until he noticed his tail and started to chase it. He got dizzier with every passing turn, spraying saliva like an oscillating lawn sprinkler.

Garfield's head made tiny circles as his eyes tracked Odie avidly. *Evolution. Go figure.*

THE MOVIE

"Garfield! Odie! Dinner!" Jon called a short while later.

Eight paws ran like thunder into the kitchen, making a beeline for Jon. Garfield wove in and out of his legs, meowing loudly, while Odie jumped and pranced in circles around both of them. Inevitably, Odie landed—*sploof!*—right on Garfield's head.

Do that once more and I'll put you through the trash compactor. Twice.

Jon set Garfield's dish down first, in its usual spot on the dining counter. Then he crossed the kitchen and put Odie's bowl on the floor next to the refrigerator. "If I were you, Odie, I'd stay clear of Garfield when he's eating. When it comes to food, Miss Manners he's not." Jon patted Odie on the head, walked out of the kitchen, and climbed the hall stairs.

Garfield chewed maybe one in ten pellets of dry food in any given meal. The rest were sucked down whole. This had been scientifically proven a number of times, usually someplace that made Jon scream, like the wool rug in the office, the red velvet sofa, or the main switching station of Jon's model railroad. Tonight, he gobbled his Kibbly Kat Krunchables faster than a mime can say nothing, and set about watching Odie address his dinner of Diddly Dawg Meaty Chunks. As he sat on the counter washing his face, Garfield noticed Odie nose a chunk out of the bowl and onto the floor, whereupon he tossed it into the air with the tip of his nose and caught it in his mouth.

What's this? Plays with his food? I'm beginning to see some advantages to this situation. Garfield hopped to the floor and sauntered over to Odie's dish. The dog cocked his head quizzically as Garfield nudged a piece of food from the bowl with a paw.

"You'll like this game, Odie. I promise. Ready? Okay, boy—fetch!" Garfield flipped the canine crouton clear across the kitchen and into the living room. While Odie scampered after it, Garfield buried his head in the bowl and scarfed a couple of chunks well before Odie returned to play some more. With a precision aim that serves to make cats downright spooky sometimes, Garfield slapped his next puck out the other door and into the den, under the table holding up the electric trains. Odie became tangled in the cloth that draped the platform, affording Garfield time to finish all of the meaty chunks but one. He took it gently in his mouth and jumped onto the counter above the dishwasher. As the sounds of *crash! sherklank! squeak, squeak (whimper, whimper, whimper)* reached him from the den, Garfield planted the dog food in the water dispenser in the refrigerator door, sat back, and waited only a second or two for Odie's return.

"Good boy! Let's try a new game now." Garfield indicated the remaining piece of kibble to Odie, who had been staring with bewilderment at his empty bowl. By this time, Jon had probably heard that last bit in the den, so Garfield would have to act fast. "Look, Odie! Here it is. Up here! All you have to do is jump for it."

Odie yipped and started to hurl himself at the refrigerator, getting higher and closer to the pellet with each vault. The thirty-two muscles of Garfield's right ear reflexively swiveled toward the sound of footsteps coming down the stairs. "Hurry, Odie! Get the Diddly Dawg!" And Odie did just that, throwing himself completely into one last leap. Just as his snout contacted the treat resting on the dispenser tray, Garfield slammed one paw against the lever, giving Odie a long, cold, filtered shower. He retracted his paw and jumped to the floor right before Jon strode angrily into the room, just in time to see Odie shake the water all over the kitchen.

The dog did it. Garfield sat by the sink and pointed.

"Odie! What are you doing?" Jon grabbed for the paper towels and dropped to the floor to blot the wood cabinets. "And what was that crash I just heard?" Other than water, the kitchen looked suspiciously tidy. Jon turned his head until he saw the disaster in the den. The entire south complex of the model railroad had plummeted to the floor, and several feet of track hung precariously over the side of the table. Jon's jaw fell and he looked back and forth between his two pets. Garfield tilted his head with the same baffled expression that was working so well for Odie.

The dog did that, too.

After dinner, Jon went to the den to put the railroad back together. Odie sat quietly in his lap as he snapped track and carefully reset the little plastic trees. Garfield flopped on his belly, propped his head up on an elbow, and watched from across the room.

"You have to learn to stay away from this stuff, Odie. I've been working for years to get everything just right. It's not *just* a railroad, it's a whole miniature shoot-'em-up cowboy town on the first transcontinental railroad. I call it 'Arbuckleville'—catchy, eh? And I'm the kingpin of this kettle," Jon said proudly, indicating the locomotive. He flipped a switch on the master control and the 4-6-2 steam locomotive whirred to life, snaking through tunnels and over bridges. Odie's head swiveled in its socket as he watched the train go around in circles.

The guy spends thousands of hours playing with trains and he can't figure out why all of his Saturday nights are free. Garfield yawned and shifted into sphinx posture.

"Look over here, boy," Jon said, pointing. "This is Main Street, with a general store and a hitching post, and this cute little water pump on the town square. No fire hydrants in those days." Jon giggled at his own joke. He was about to press a button on the transformer when Odie lifted his head and licked his hand affectionately. "Whoa there, little fella! That soggy tongue of yours is going to get us both electrocuted." He took Odie by the ears and nuzzled his face.

This is definitely one of those nights when I'll have to lose my dinner, but I'll wait until after Jon goes to sleep and leave it by the side of his bed.

"Maybe it's time to turn in, anyway," Jon yawned. "What a day we've all had! Why, it's the first day of the rest of our lives together!"

Garfield groaned. *Friday night, 9:47. Jon Arbuckle's personal best, folks; he's really flirting with the edge this time. Dust off the record books.*

"Garfield, did you have any idea when we woke up this morning that our lives would change forever by lunchtime?"

Jon, did you have any idea when you woke up this morning that your sudden and mysterious demise would leap to the top of my to-do list? Jon left the den and walked up the stairs with Odie tripping at his heels. Garfield held back with a very cross expression on his face. *And did somebody mention lunch?*

* * *

THE MOVIE

Later, Garfield crawled into his kitty bed and hugged Pooky twice. It had been a two-hug day. *Our lives are ruined, Pooky. Why did Liz do this to me? Doesn't she like me anymore? Have I done something to offend? I think she must have Jon under some kind of spell.* He kneaded the pillows, turned a few circles, and dropped into optimal sleeping position. He rested his chin on his front paws and gazed across the room at Odie, who was frolicking on Jon's bed.

If I were you, dodo boy, I'd grab some rug. The floor tends to get cold at night.

Odie buried his head under the covers, stuck his tail in the air, and wiggled his butt. Here was temptation the likes of which Garfield could not resist. He leapt lightly to the end table, extended an arm, and launched the alarm clock straight at the business end of the fox-trotting dog. Odie yelped and jumped, burrowing deeper until he disappeared altogether under the blanket. Garfield heard the water stop running in the bathroom sink, and quickly made for his side of the room. He took the canine route, launching himself off the wriggling lump. Pooky cushioned his landing back on his own bed, where Garfield curled up and said, "I'll make you a deal, Odie."

This was greeted by a muffled whimper.

"I'll try being nicer if you try being smarter."

Jon walked in from the bathroom in his striped pajamas, rubbing floss back and forth between his teeth.

Hey, new kid. Be on the lookout for UFOs.

Jon melted when he saw Odie tangled in the sheets. "It seems somebody has turned down my bed for me!" He trashed the floss and smiled as he took the alarm clock off the bed and restored it to the end table.

"Where's Odie?" he said in an exaggerated voice. "Hey, Garfield—have you seen Odie?"

Would that I hadn't.

"Why, I can't find him anywhere! Wherever could he be?" Under the covers, Odie's tail went *thump, thump, thump*. Jon jumped on the bed and yanked off the blanket, grabbing Odie playfully by the ears. "You want to sleep with me? Isn't that sweet! We can keep each other warm."

Garfield rolled his eyes and began to wonder why he ever wanted his own little bed in the first place.

"What a good boy!" Jon straightened the bedding, stepped out of his bunny slippers, and climbed in next to Odie, scratching his belly and whispering in his ear. Odie licked Jon across the lips.

I think I'm going to blow cat chow.

Jon leaned over and switched off the light. Garfield crawled under his covers, defeated. That night, Garfield dreamt that Odie turned into a giant hot dog, which he ate. With mustard, sauerkraut, and—last but not least—*relish*. He slept with a smile on his face.

After breakfast the next morning, Garfield sat on the porch. Odie sat next to him, wagging his tail, lolling his tongue, and gawking at Garfield expectantly.

Don't look at me.

The newsboy rolled by on his bike and tossed the paper onto the Arbuckle lawn. Odie forgot Garfield and dashed off the porch to retrieve it. The dog hesitated for a moment, torn between chasing the bicycle and bringing the paper home. He plucked the paper from the walk and trotted back proudly, happily thrashing his head back and forth and sometimes beaning himself with the paper. Jon met him at the front door as he pranced up the porch steps.

"Odie! You got my newspaper!" He boxed playfully with the dog, and gently lifted the burden from his mouth. "In all these years, Garfield has never gotten my paper. I'm lucky if he doesn't shred it. Good fella!" He turned to the cat in question, not at all pleased. "As for *you*, no more waking presents by the side of my bed, got it?" Jon went into the house and sat down to catch up on the news.

"Good fella!" Garfield mocked, his eyes narrowing. *Suck-up.* He jumped off the porch and headed down the driveway, tucking himself under Jon's car to have a long think. Wedging twenty-some-odd pounds of pure fat under a ton and a half of Detroit's finest was like trying to stuff a turkey with a football.

After a while, Garfield saw the milk truck pull up to the curb. *Too much thinking. I need to eat. Eat liquid meat.* He started the long wiggle out from under the muffler. Odie bounced into view with a ball in his mouth and his ears flopping. Garfield ignored him, heading for the porch and the fresh bottles the milkman had just left.

Odie knocked Garfield over from behind and dropped the ball on his nose, wagging his tail and panting.

"Hey, what are you doing? Leave me alone!"

Odie looked at Garfield blankly and nudged the ball forward with his muzzle.

"I'm not kidding, Dodie Odie. Take a chill pill and get lost. I'm busy." *Where is Nermal when I need him?* Garfield turned to scan the block. Odie grabbed the ball and circled him. Once more, he dropped the ball at Garfield's feet.

"You want to play? Fine. Make yourself useful and get in the pail."

Odie stayed put, looking at Garfield expectantly.

"Do I have to do everything around here?" Garfield stuck out a paw and batted the ball into the bucket. "C'mon, Odie. We'll play the ball's-in-the-pail game. You'll love it."

Odie sat and stared at Garfield.

"I'd explain it to you, but your head would explode. Let me show you." Garfield pointed with his right paw. "Ball. Pail. Fetch. Do I have to spell it out for you? Can I be more clear?"

Odie cocked his head, which sent his ears flapping.

Garfield rolled his eyes and jumped in the bucket to show Odie, who suddenly remembered his legs and backed into the wind chimes swinging from above. The chimes struck a potted plant that raised a string that pulled on a lever that lifted the pail that seesawed a plank that sent everything flying, including Garfield. A bottle of milk slid down the plank and began to teeter, hanging on until Garfield landed on his back, mouth open, directly underneath. *CRASH!* The airborne pail got there first, covering Garfield. Overhead, he could hear the sound of all of that lovely milk sloshing into the pail, followed by the unmistakable *glug-glug* of Odie's slurping. The dog licked the pail clean and trotted off.

"Very funny, Odie!" came the voice from under the bucket. "You're a real laugh riot! Well, I've got another game we can play. It's called the MY-CLAW-IN-YOUR-BOOTY game. Remember that one from yesterday? I'll go first." Garfield threw the pail over and tore across the street after the unsuspecting Odie, who was taking a fire hydrant for a test run.

Arlene and Nermal had seen the entire incident from her driveway.

"Gee, Nermal," Arlene said thoughtfully. "When is the

last time you saw Garfield run for anything other than a meal?"

"Nope," he agreed. "You don't get to see *this* every day."

Garfield was closing in on his target. "Ramming speed!" he shouted, and stepped up the chase. Odie took off.

"No, Garfield! Don't!" Arlene tried to stop him, for only she and Nermal could see where the wee tan mutt was leading him.

Garfield almost had Odie when Luca stepped into his path, grinning maniacally. Garfield skidded to a stop and, with a sinking feeling, realized what had happened. He had run straight into Luca's yard, and there was no way out.

Garfield stood up, cleared his throat, and slapped a big grin on his face. "Good morning, ladies and germs! I just flew in from up the block and boy, are my arms tired! Hey, what do you call a cow with two legs? *Lean beef!* And speaking of beef, what do you call a cow with *no* legs? GROUND beef! Ha ha ha! Speaking of no legs, what do you call a *dog* with no legs? You don't! He can't come anyway! Ha ha ha ha ha ha ha!"

Not even Nermal and Arlene were laughing. Garfield gulped hard.

"Well, well, well. If it isn't Shamu's stunt double, taking up comedy," snarled the Doberman.

"Hey, Shamu was a *nobody* before he put on weight," Garfield retorted.

Luca licked his chops. "I've finally got you trapped, cat. I've been waiting *years* for this moment."

Garfield swallowed. "Uhhh, regular years or dog years?" He backed away slowly from the intolerable dog breath. Then he tripped and became hopelessly tangled in a garden hose. Luca stepped closer, his teeth bared. He hovered over the helpless feline and spread his jaws wide, ready to chomp down on his quarry. Across the street, Nermal and Arlene looked on. She was shaking the tiniest bit.

Fhoom! To everyone's surprise, Odie bounced between Luca and his next meal. Characteristically oblivious to Garfield's predicament, Odie barked and nuzzled Luca playfully. Luca took a swipe at the new dog and wrestled him to the ground.

Odie was enjoying himself immensely.

Luca started to circle, and Odie stood up and followed suit. Noses to butts, they inspected each other in that secret, disgusting way dogs have. Garfield saw his opportunity and scampered off to join Arlene and Nermal, watching from the sidelines.

Garfield proceeded to lick a paw and wash behind his ears. "I've got one word for that dog. *Decaf.*"

"*What* is your problem?" Arlene was very annoyed. "If it wasn't for Odie, you'd be Luca's chew toy right now."

"Yeah," agreed Nermal. "He saved your hide. Odie's a hero."

"Odie's an *imbecile*," Garfield said, bored.

The three cats watched Luca and Odie wrestle and nip at one another. Odie especially enjoyed head-butting the much larger dog in the leg from a running start, until Luca wised up, lay down, and sent Odie somersaulting over his back and lurching into a hydrangea bush. Luca sneezed in the ticklish shower of pale blue petals.

"They seem to like each other," Nermal observed. "Odie's making new friends already."

"Water seeks its own level," Garfield said drily. "They can start a local chapter of Droolers Anonymous."

Odie was down on his stomach, crawling submissively toward the big black dog.

"Odie thinks Luca is cool."

"Error of semantics, Nermal. Never use 'Odie' and 'thinks' in the same sentence." Garfield watched the Doberman knock a gazing ball from its stone perch, something for which Luca was sure to catch it later from Pack Leader. The dogs began to play nose soccer in and out of the garden gnomes. As always, Luca's chain followed him wherever he went. Three kitty heads tracked in unison.

"I don't know if I can bear to watch," Arlene moaned, turning her head.

"This is an accident waiting to happen," said Nermal, wincing.

"I detect another benefit to having the mutt around the house," Garfield said, looking skyward and ticking off two fingers on his left paw. "More food up for grabs, and he can keep Luca off my back."

"I'm leaving," Arlene announced curtly. "It stinks of ingratitude around here." With that, she turned in a dramatic huff and stormed off.

"You know you can't stay away from irresistible me for long!" he called after her.

"Oh, yeah? You're not the only cat in the clowder. Just watch me!" she shot back.

He cupped a forefoot around his lips and shouted, "After you've dated old 'Passion Paws,' no one else will do!"

"Gee, I don't know, Garfield," Nermal offered. "Puddles Ziccardi told me she saw Arlene by the fence with Buzzsaw the other night."

Garfield's eyes widened. "Buzzsaw? That *sissy*? Why, he's . . . he's . . . *declawed*!"

"C'mon, Nermal," Arlene shouted back. "We were on our way to go through the Osbornes' trash. They had that big cookout last weekend, remember? Let's go."

"See ya, Garfield. I'm a sucker for the call of the wild spare rib." Nermal bounded adorably after Arlene.

Garfield watched them disappear down the block, kicked the bucket, and then twisted his way angrily through the pet door and into the house. Even the thought that he'd made short work of the Osborne barbecue hours ago failed to lighten his mood.

Chapter Six

After lunch, Garfield was spread out on the Sacred Chair, digesting and napping. Jon had gone downtown to meet with the sprinkler people, and the house was silent except for Odie's soft snoring in the entryway. The supple feline stretched luxuriously in his sleep and turned his head until it was upside down on the chair. His eyes opened slightly, and in that split second his ears picked up the distinctive whistle of a substitute mailman approaching the house. The regular carrier *must* have been on vacation, because Garfield had terrorized him long ago into leaving the mail as quickly and quietly as possible, or else.

A thick stack of letters and magazines came shooting through the mail slot in the door, bomping the snoozing dog on the nose and waking him abruptly. Garfield opened his eyes fully and turned to watch as Odie attacked the day's delivery, thrashing his head and chewing up envelopes. A free disc good for seven million free hours in a month of online service shot like a Frisbee into the den, landing on the Arbuckleville Town Square. Odie grabbed a magazine between his teeth and shook it back and forth until he started to sneeze from the perfume sample bound in the pages.

GARFIELD

That had better not be my subscription to Cat Fancy. *I wonder how to set the laser printer to "stun."*

Odie lay down in the confetti to eat the telephone bill. Garfield picked up the remote control and commenced channel surfing. "Washington insiders confirmed today that the President suffered minor injuries when he slipped on a banana peel at a ceremony dedicating the new monkey house at the National Zoo . . ." *Click!* "Don't touch that dial! Dr. Phil will be back right after the break to humiliate you some more! . . ." *Click!* "Rats: Are they just big mice?". . . *Click!* "I'm leaving you, Marsha, because you're a selfish little vixen who never thinks about anyone but herself . . ."

Click! "Welcome back to Dancin' Fools TV, television you can shake a leg at! Check out the oldie but goodie we have for you today!" Garfield settled into the chair and fixed his attention on the sprightly music video as it flickered across the screen. While tapping his paw along to the music would have been too taxing, his tail did sort of carry the rhythm.

Odie jumped onto the chair and hunkered down next to Garfield. A postage stamp was stuck to his lower lip.

"No." Garfield wasted no time shoving Odie to the floor. "Get lost. I'm busy right now." Odie wasted no time climbing right back up onto the chair, and wagged his tail.

Garfield turned to Odie and asked coolly, "What part of 'no' don't you understand? I don't want to play. I want to *veg*, as in 'quality TV time.' " Once more, Garfield pushed the dog to the floor. Once more, Odie scrambled back up and yipped with the joy of the game.

"ODIE! Stop it. What do you want me to say, 'Thanks for saving my hide with Luca'? Fine. *Thanks*. There, I've said it. Now leave me alone."

Odie snuggled closer, panting happily.

66

THE MOVIE

Garfield got a wicked look in his eye, picked up a pillow with his teeth, and nailed the poor dog on the head. Odie tumbled to the floor. Garfield smiled, savoring his victory. *That ought to show this nitwit just who's boss around here. That'll teach him to stay off my chair.*

The moment didn't last long, however, because Odie came right back at him with a pillow of his own. As the song coming from the television grew louder, an all-out pillow fight was taking shape. "Shake, shake, shake your paw-aw-aw . . ." *Kaboing! Bonk! Oooof!* "Wag, wag, wag that tai-ai-ail!" *Thwack! Glonk! Splush!*

Garfield really wanted to hate Odie. He wanted to punish him for ruining the perfect life he had carefully built with Jon all these years. The problem was, every time he knocked Odie down, Odie would bounce right back up, grinning and giving as good as he got. Garfield caught himself smiling. There was something kind of appealing in such innocent stupidity. Despite himself, Garfield was having fun.

The music took over. Before he even knew it, The G was spinning, moonwalking, and shaking his proverbial money-maker, and Odie was joyfully imitating every smooth move. They wrestled and they danced. Garfield baited Odie with a laugh. "Missed me! Missed me! Now you've got to kiss me!" Together they boogied across the living room and out the front door, spilling onto the porch. They tumbled and played in the glorious sunshine.

That is, until Garfield caught sight of Nermal, Arlene, and Luca watching them from the far curb. Garfield screeched to a halt and punted Odie clear across the lawn, adding, "And *stay* out!" loudly enough for the spectators to hear. He sat down on the porch and began to lick himself with great concentration.

GARFIELD

Liz pulled her pickup truck into the driveway and beeped the horn. As Jon emerged from the house, he spotted Odie mindlessly rolling around on the grass. "Odie! There you are. C'mon, we've got a date with Liz." He could barely contain his excitement as he scooped Odie up and hopped into Liz's pickup truck. He slammed the door behind them.

Nermal sidled over to the porch. "Hey, Garfield. Jon's taking Odie on his date with Liz and leaving you behind."

"I know, Mr. States-the-Obvious."

"They're off on an adventure and you're still here."

"And your point is . . . ?"

"Well, that's got to feel bad, being left by Jon while he takes Odie out. It's like you're not his favorite anymore." Nermal was catching on incredibly fast, for Nermal.

"I get the picture, Nermal. Hey, why don't you have a nice day, somewhere else?" The Siamese kitten suddenly got interested in a fly, and Garfield turned away to conceal the desperation and jealousy he felt. Nermal followed the fly off the porch, leaving Garfield alone to face the truth about his feelings.

This isn't happening to me. I've been replaced by the dumbest dog on the planet—dumber, even, than Luca. I cannot sit back and do nothing—though, granted, that works for me ninety percent of the time. Odie would put a stamp on an e-mail. That is Anna Nicole *stupid! I've got to show Jon just how stupid stupid is.*

The pickup backed out of the driveway. Garfield leapt off the porch and ran toward the truck. Liz shifted gears and the truck did a forward turn. With a final burst of energy, Garfield hurled himself at the bumper, hooking his claws at the moment of contact.

THE MOVIE

The truck rolled down the street toward the corner. Garfield was barely hanging on, and his rotund form bounced along the pavement as he clung for dear life. Inch by painful inch, "Indiana" Garfield used all of his might to pull himself up onto the ledge. Summoning strength he didn't know he had, he flung himself over the rim and onto the flatbed, landing with a painful thud. Flat on his back and breathing hard, Garfield wondered if the time wasn't right to join up at Curves for Cats.

Extremely self-satisfied, he sat up and shook himself, making flapping noises with his ears. Then he settled in for a bath. Liz suddenly hit the brakes on the pickup and—*THWOMP!*—Garfield went flying into the rear window, paws splayed.

Inside the cab, nobody noticed the huge blob of choice kitty slamming into the glass only inches from their heads. Liz was too upset and Jon was too besotted. "Whoa!" Liz cried. "Did you see that squirrel dart into the street? I can't believe how close I came to hitting it!"

Garfield's face flattened as he slid down the glass just behind them, landing with a *yeow!* on the cold corrugated metal of the flatbed.

"You have excellent reflexes, Liz," Jon said. "I like that in a wo—veterinarian."

Liz took her foot off the brake and relaxed as they drove on through sun-dappled streets. "So how's Garfield taking it?" she asked.

"Taking what?"

"Odie. How's Garfield handling having a dog around?" Her face wore a look of concern.

Not very well. Garfield sat up and could see Odie on the seat between them, misting the windshield.

"I think it's going pretty well so far, actually. There hasn't been any blood yet."

Liz smiled at the news. "I'm very relieved to hear you say that, Jon. It's not always easy to put a dog and a cat together under one roof, and Garfield's had you all to himself for so long. I knew *you* would be great for Odie, but I wasn't one hundred percent sure this would work out."

Jon gave a little wave of his hand. "You know Garfield. Nothing really bothers him."

Oh, where shall I begin in my quest to disabuse you of your ignorance?

A short while later, the truck pulled into a parking lot. Liz found a space along the curb near the expansive lawn abutting the building.

"Isn't this a no-parking zone?" Jon asked Liz, looking up and down the lane and pointing to the signs.

"Not when you're one of the judges," she giggled, reaching into her purse for her official blue ribbon. She pinned it to the lapel of her hot-pink blazer.

"Wow, I'm impressed," Jon said admiringly. He snapped Odie's leash onto his collar. "What do you say to that, boy? We're here with a genuine VIP!" Odie barked with delight as they jumped from the car and strolled toward the lawn, which was alive with activity. Garfield climbed out of the flatbed just in time to see them pass through a makeshift entrance into a fenced-off area surrounded by tables, tents, and bleachers. Jon, Liz, and Odie instantly disappeared into the enormous crowd that milled about on the other side of the ropes.

What in the name of the known universe is going on here? Who knew there were so many people? Garfield

70

had never seen this many humans at once. He jumped down from the truck and started toward the spot where he'd lost sight of his traveling companions, but was scared of all of the people crowding the entrance. He skirted the temporary fence, looking for another way in.

As if on cue, a union guy rolled by with a cloth-covered trolley heaped with glossy ribbons and one giant, sparkling trophy.

Aha! Public transportation! Wait up! Garfield made a run for it, springing through the drapes and settling on the lower shelf of the cart. Not being able to see where they were going was a small price to pay for the free ride, and there was a roll of tape to play with for the duration. Eventually the cart squeaked to a stop. Garfield poked his nose through the tablecloth and found himself enclosed in a green-and-white tent filled with boxes of paper and stacks of folding chairs.

He picked his way across the grass floor of the tent and poked his nose out the other side. In front of him was a long table at which sat five people talking quietly among themselves. One of them was Liz, but Jon and Odie were nowhere in sight. He ducked under Liz's chair and between her legs, scooted under the table, and puzzled over how they might have gotten separated.

If Garfield had been able to see the large sign hoisted over the table under which he sat, he'd have hitched the next trophy cart right back out to the parking lot. Printed on the sign, in big white letters, were the words PAN TING DOG SHOW.

Liz unbuttoned her jacket and shifted in her seat at the judging dais. She shared the responsibility with the local television personality Happy Chapman, sitting to her left, and Miss Ace Hardware, who sat on the other side of Happy and was basking in the celebrity splendor of the Kibbly Kat pitchman.

"I just want to say," she squeaked, as excited as she could be, "I am such a big fan of yours! I watch your show every day!" She placed her hand on top of his.

"Thank you," he said, clearly bored. He pushed his wide-brimmed hat a little lower on his forehead, and smoothed the lapels of his double-breasted navy sports jacket.

Liz kept one ear on the conversation as she dutifully organized her papers and number-two pencils. "I've wanted to meet you for a very long time . . ." crooned Miss Ace Hardware. "In person. In the flesh."

"Here I am," Happy replied, his voice flat.

The gushing continued. "I can't believe I'm actually sitting next to *Walter J. Chapman*!"

Happy turned to face the beauty queen and clenched his teeth. "I think you're confusing me with my *brother*," he spat. "I'm *Happy* Chapman!"

"No, you're not. Happy Chapman is the guy in the hideous orange safari suit with that disgusting cat," Miss Ace Hardware replied, absolutely sure of herself.

"Oh, I couldn't agree more," Happy snorted.

"Excuse me, Mr. Chapman," Liz interjected politely. "I just wanted to introduce myself. I'm Liz Wilson, a vet here in town. My patients and I really enjoy your work on the *Mello in the Morning* show. I mean, when I get to see it. I'm usually working at that time."

Miss Ace Hardware sat back, the smile vanishing from her face. "Oh. Right. That guy on channel thirty-seven." Now it was her turn to be bored. She took out a nail file and proceeded to inspect her manicure.

A voiced boomed over the loudspeakers. "Welcome, ladies, gentlemen, and canines, to the annual dog show sponsored by Pan Ting Grooming Products! Remember, folks, looks *are* everything! Make your dog's coat zing with Pan Ting!" The announcer chortled at his own fine delivery. "Now, before we get started, I'd like to take a moment to introduce today's distinguished panel of judges. First, Miss Ace Hardware, Misty Stutterheim!"

The crowd applauded enthusiastically, offering the odd whistle and catcall. These were likely inspired by Miss Ace Hardware's outfit, a somewhat fabric-free ensemble consisting of tiny white shorts, a pert red tank top, her pageant sash, and nothing else. Misty stood up, flashing a dazzling smile and a shiny new circular saw, and threw kisses to the crowd. An entire section of men woofed in unison.

"Now let's give a warm welcome to Mister Happy himself, Happy Chapman!" Happy got up, waved, and cried "Remember . . . *be happy!*"—his trademarked motto, in which the boisterous throng was only too eager to join him. The audience togetherness set off a human wave. The applause was so loud that Liz's introduction was heard by no one, which was just as well, since just about no one had heard of her. Though very pretty, her red dress and tailored pink blazer were no competition for the sartorial appeal of Miss Ace Hardware.

"We've got a full, exciting day ahead of us," the announcer continued, "so sit back, relax, and remember: It's not the dog in the fight, it's the fight in the dog!" A group of rather large gentlemen with shiny pink faces started shaking their fists and yelling "Whoo! Whoo! Whoo!" from the bottoms of their throats. They all wore the same T-shirt, which featured a slobbering bulldog head in a spiked collar.

Up in the stands, Jon and Odie got comfortable in their seats. Jon opened his program and read aloud to Odie about the various classes of competition. Odie was hanging on Jon's every word, which of course reached him as no more than "Blah, blah, Odie. Blah, blah, blah, Odie."

Under the judges' table, Garfield poked his head out the side and craned his neck to get a better look, but his view was completely obscured by an enormous topiary planted nearby.

Well beyond the bush was a stand of bleachers heaving with people. *Maybe Jon and Odie are over there.* He inched out into the open and then sprinted for the nearest potted plant, where he took a moment to plot his next move. All of these people were a little unnerving, and Garfield was feeling overwhelmed. He darted, serpentine-style, from plant to table to tent, ducking behind each until he was sure he hadn't been spotted.

He remained blissfully unaware of the event unfolding in the main arena.

I know I'm on the trail. I can smell that stinking, dribbling mutt, well, everywhere! I've probably been just a few steps behind them this whole time! Garfield's ears swiveled madly to the dozens of voices and conversations drifting overhead from the scaffold.

"My Waffles—his full name is Sir Parsifal Faerie Frolic of Waffledom—he still has bed-wetting issues . . . Did you hear about Mr. Deeds? So tragic, that business with the electric clippers . . . No, Odie, don't chew the program . . ."

Ah-ha! Garfield crept out from behind the tent and walked in front of the stands, searching the sea of faces that stretched up to the blue sky. His body was tense and he sought cover under a small table. He spotted Jon and the mutt seated in the bleachers, not far from where he sat. From this vantage point, he tried discreetly to get Odie's attention.

"Hey . . . Odie! Yo!" Garfield whispered. Garfield tried again, louder this time. "*Psssst.* C'mere, Odie. COME HERE, you stupid . . ."

And just as that final word left his lips, Garfield looked up and noticed, for the first time, that he was in a gigantic enclosure that *reeked* of . . .

". . . *dog,*" he said weakly.

A few dogs noticed and buzzed among themselves. Garfield *and* the fur on his back rose slowly. He bonked his head on the underside of the table. *What an ugly piece of furniture. Such spindly legs.* He started to inch backward, away from the dogs and toward the bleachers. *And why do they . . . MOVE??*

Just then, the "table" dropped its head to take a good look at Garfield, who found himself eye to eye with the upside-down face of a large Doberman. He was even bigger and meaner-looking than Luca. Garfield's stomach left town. It occurred to him that it might be prudent for the rest of him to follow.

"*Achtung,* baby," he said, trying and failing to grin.

He turned around, and everywhere Garfield looked, dogs came into focus and were beginning to smell cat. They glared, growled, and snorted, and passed the news along to the other dogs. A few of the larger ones pawed the ground. The little dogs yipped. The mob started to drift in Garfield's direction.

Garfield threw back his head and howled, a dark, low

note that sounded more bovine than feline. *Hey! You up there! Pack leaders! Mind your dogs, would ya?*

The humans were too engrossed in their own dramas to notice what was happening. Garfield inched backward until his flashing tail brushed across something solid. From the corner of his eye he saw the distinct jowls of a rottweiler, a breed just as terrifying as the Doberman, only twice as broad across.

Garfield smiled weakly. "Arf?" Rather than wait for a response, the terrified kitty bolted into the middle of the arena. He scurried under a large canvas sign spread out on the grass.

By now every dog was mobilized. They broke away from their handlers and tore after the quivering orange pincushion that was Garfield.

"Baskerville! . . . Prudence! . . . Jasper! . . . Bubbles!"

There was bedlam in the house. The shouts of the crowd were drowned out by the sound of a thousand doggy yelps as the four-legged ran toward the gelatinous lump under the canvas with but a single thought: GET CAT NOW.

The announcer tried to instill order. "Everybody! Please maintain control of your dogs!"

Nobody listened.

"People! Please!" The people were running after the dogs. The announcer took a handkerchief from his pocket and started to mop his brow.

Garfield wiggled out from under the canvas and spotted a path. He dashed among the tangle of canine bodies and broke through, heading for the other side of the bleachers. The pack of dogs, moving as one leggy, floppy-eared mass, followed in hot pursuit.

The announcer was gulping something from a small

flask and quickly losing his composure. "Ladies and gen . . . ohhh, forget it. *You!*" he shouted, snapping his fingers at a technician. "Music! *Now!*"

A rollicking tune blasted suddenly from every arena-sized loudspeaker surrounding the grassy field. Odie cocked his head in recognition and perked up. It was the same song that had been playing on the television that morning at home. While Garfield led all the other dogs out of the main area and down a narrow passage, Odie leapt from Jon's arms, ran to the center of the ring, and started to boogie.

Just as Garfield had taught him at home, Odie bumped, shimmied, and wiggled in time to the music. He got up on his hind legs, shook his ears, and howled with the pleasure of the dance. *Step, kick, step, kick, shimmy shimmy bop!* Jon stared at his simple dog in utter astonishment. Not for one minute did he ever think Odie had it in him.

Jon wasn't the only one who noticed. The entire crowd was cheering him on. Over at the judges' table, Liz dropped her pencil in surprise and her mouth hung open. Miss Ace Hardware continued to examine her fingernails. Happy Chapman watched Odie intently. "Talented little fella," he said, to no one in particular. *"Ah . . . ah . . . ahhh CHOO!"* Happy wiped his nose on his judge's ribbon and began to think very hard about the engaging dog cutting a rug in the center ring.

Garfield leapt over a podium at top speed and skidded to a halt in what proved to be the grooming area. He saw a round fluffy woman carefully placing a round fluffy dog into a cage. He could hear the rabble behind him, and it was closing in fast. With a running leap, Garfield made for the woman and skittered under her voluminous dress. He clawed his way up her back and wiggled behind the zipper.

The woman twisted and thrashed her arms in every direction, trying in vain to throw off her unseen assailant. She chased her back in much the same way that Odie chased his tail. As she spun toward the passageway, she saw a wall of fangs, drool, and doggy determination heading straight for her at thirty-five miles per hour. She screamed and took off, hounded by the dogs.

Garfield popped his head out of the dress at the neckline. He bounced and swayed as the woman ran, but she was no match for the pack of fit show dogs. Garfield saw them gaining on him, and began to beg.

"Look, guys. I'm with you. I mean, I cried at the end of *Sounder*."

Unimpressed, the dogs started to leap for Garfield and snap at the hem of the woman's dress. She threw up her hands and dashed around a corner, where . . . *WHAM!* She ran smack into a posse of dog owners heading in her direction. The short stop sent Garfield flying over the mob of humans. Following his arc, the dogs leapt after him.

What no one had anticipated was the neatly stacked display of dog food waiting for them on the other side. *STRIKE! Crash!* One cat and dozens of dogs scattered the pile of cans like just so many bowling pins.

Garfield sat up and shook himself conscious. Dogs were recovering all around him. He dashed off again, with the pack hot on his heels. The few people who weren't tangled in the heap behind the dog food stared in amazement as they saw only the very tippy-top of a furry ginger tail whiz past a row of open cages, followed by the gang of slavering dogs.

THE MOVIE

Up ahead, Garfield saw his premature demise in the form of a dead end. The dogs were getting closer. Garfield skidded to a halt and turned to face them.

"Stop!" he yelled, holding up a paw.

Surprisingly, they all did.

"Look!" Garfield shouted, gesturing wildly. "The FedEx guy!" In one Pavlovian turn of the head, all of the dogs looked in the direction in which Garfield had pointed. It gave him just the time he needed to skirt the throng and break away.

The smarter among them realized they'd been had, and led the dumber dogs in resuming the chase. Garfield shot through a hole in the fence and up a tree, flinching at the yelps and whimpers of dogs that started to collect at the base of the trunk. The shaking orange cat leaned his back against a limb, his breath coming in sputtering gasps. He looked down to see the parking lot stretching out before him. Safety at last.

"The thing about dog shows is . . ." *pant, pant* ". . . they're all wild, dim-witted, uncontrollable beasts, but one of them gets a blue ribbon." Garfield wheezed some more, and then noticed a miniature dachshund attached by his teeth to his tail.

Garfield shook off the wiener (plop! *arf!arf!arf!*) and hid in the leaves while owners ran out to collect their dogs and lead them back to the show ring. Once the coast was clear, Garfield shimmied headfirst down the bark, landing with an unceremonious thud in a patch of clover. He shuddered and settled in the grass, waiting for his heartbeat to slow down to normal. Then he walked back to the parking lot and hunkered down under Liz's truck, taking advantage of the shade and waiting to catch the ride home. He promptly fell into a deep sleep.

Back in the main arena, the dogs calmed and the competition began. Working and sporting dogs, toys, terriers, and more went through their paces, until the time had come for the final category, "Outstanding Dog in the Mutt Class."

Odie was back in the stands, snoozing in Jon's lap and dreaming happily of his new orange friend. Jon was daydreaming about Liz, and couldn't take his eyes off her as she conferred quietly with the other judges. Finally, Happy Chapman stood up, took the microphone from the announcer, and walked to the podium in front of the table.

"Ladies and gentlemen, it is time to announce our last, but hardly least, winner of this year's competition. I know one little diddly doggy that's certainly earned his meaty chunks today. Let's have a warm round of applause for . . . *Odie!*" The applause was more wild than warm. The crowd started chanting, *"Ohhh-die! Ohhh-die! Ohhh-die!"* That's what it took to snap Jon from his daydreams and the dog from his nap. Jon leapt up in amazement, leading a groggy Odie to the winner's circle.

Happy placed the blue ribbon around Odie's neck, carefully avoiding the hot breath of the perpetually panting dog. He shook Jon's hand warmly, and the other judges came over to join them. Miss Ace Hardware posed for the crowd. Liz and Jon stood side by side, gazing proudly at Odie. Odie chewed on the ribbon. His teeth were turning blue.

"You've got some smart dog there," Happy said to Jon, over all the cheering. "Acrobatic, obedient, theatrical . . . He could have a future in television."

"Smart? Odie?"

THE MOVIE

"Happy Chapman doesn't lie." He leaned in to Jon and lowered his voice. "In fact, I'm always looking for a dog with Odie's unique abilities."

Jon stooped to smoosh Odie on the head. "Sorry," he said, making kissy faces with the dog. "I'm not interested. Odie's my pet and that's all I want him to be." Odie let out a sunny yelp and licked Jon on the lips.

Happy was disappointed. "Suit yourself. But if you change your mind, just give ol' Happy a call." He handed Jon a business card. A photographer signaled to them to pose, and Happy laid on his most winning smile just as the flash went off.

Chapter Seven

Garfield awoke with a start to the sound of the ignition turning over. The truck slowly rolled away from the curb, exposing the groggy cat to the brilliant sunshine. *My ride!* He ran for the pickup and grabbed on to the exhaust pipe. Liz gained speed as she pulled into the lane, and Garfield wrapped his tail and all four legs around the duct, silently promising somebody somewhere that if he survived this, he would always be a very good cat from now on.

As they approached the exit, they passed Happy's S-class Mercedes, which was hard to miss due to its license plate, BE HAPPY. Jon, who had been chattering excitedly about the day's events, noticed the car. "Happy Chapman's a lot taller in real life than he appears on television. And he seemed so taken with Odie, didn't he? That arena was filled with purebred show dogs, and Odie showed them *all* a thing or two! Didn't you, boy?" He scratched Odie behind the ears. Odie's tail went *thump, thump, thump* in Liz's lap.

"I've got to admit," said Liz, with admiration, "I've never seen anything quite like it."

"Did you hear that, Odie?" Odie *had* heard, but didn't understand a word of it. "Not even Liz has seen anything like it!" Jon hugged his talented little hoofer lovingly. "I don't like to brag," he started, using one of those phrases that becomes a lie as soon as it gets said, "but I *do* think I provide a secure, loving home, and my pets seem to thrive." He glanced at Liz with what he hoped was a modest smile. She smiled back. They reached the edge of the parking lot and waited for the traffic light to signal them onto the main road.

Meanwhile, under the truck, a less-than-thriving Garfield was beginning to sweat as the exhaust pipe grew warmer. If he stayed where he was for the entire trip, he might as well be a cat on a spit, certain to fry in his own fat. From the corner of his eye he saw the pavement begin to move as Liz steered the truck out of the lot. Valiantly defying gravity, the terrified feline shimmied upside down toward the daylight until his front paws hit rubber. *Sproing!* He dug into the bumper with all ten claws. Taking a deep breath, Garfield tried to talk himself into releasing his hind legs and tail from around the exhaust pipe. *O claws, which have served me well with the neighborhood dogs and certain vacuum-packed grocery items over the years, if ever you are to work your magic, let it be now.*

Garfield shut his eyes, tensed his arms, and let his hind-quarters free-fall. *OOOOF!* His feet hit asphalt and reflexively started running to keep up with the truck as it pulled ahead of him. It was no use. Clinging desperately to the bumper, Garfield skied along the avenue on his paunch. Under other circumstances, he might have enjoyed it as a very nice belly rub. If only the world weren't zipping by so nauseatingly *fast*.

Mercifully, the truck rolled to a stop at the next corner.

Garfield hurled himself onto the bumper and over the tail-gate, landing with the heaviest of thuds on the cold, corrugated flatbed. He lay on his back, his paws in the air, breathing hard and waiting for the sky to stop spinning.

Never leave the house. Never, ever leave the house.

Liz pulled the pickup into Jon's driveway and braked to a gentle stop. Jon gathered all his courage and turned to face the vet of his dreams. "I had a really fun time. Thank you."

Liz smiled demurely and said, "Me, too."

Emboldened, Jon's voice grew eager. "Would you like to come in?"

"Not today," she said.

Thwomp! went the sound of Jon's heart. "I knew that. Sorry." He turned to look out the window, hoping Liz wouldn't notice his disappointment.

But she did notice, and quickly added, "Jon, I'd love to come over, just not today. I have to cover for another vet."

"Oh," Jon replied dully. Then he realized what she'd actually said, and his voice brightened. "Really?"

"Really," Liz smiled. "How's Sunday?"

"Sunday's good!" Jon could barely mask his astonishment. *Did Liz really want to see him again?* He was unaccustomed to seeing the same person twice, and had an unusually high incidence of women leaving the country the day after the first date. This was news. Jon couldn't wait to tell Garfield. He sang his good-byes, beckoned Odie, and waved until Liz and her truck were safely down the block and out of sight. Then he did a happy dance and skipped all the way to the front door.

* * *

While the humans talked in the truck, Garfield dropped to the ground, righted himself, and tried to shake off the ride. His head was still vibrating as he staggered toward the house.

He turned to take one last look at the pickup. Jon and Liz seemed lost in conversation and did not notice his vast orange magnificence in the least. A scruffy tan tail popped in and out of the picture like a windshield wiper. With a heavy sigh, Garfield squeezed through the kitty door, sat down, and put his head in his paws.

Why? Why? Why? I'm supposed to be his favorite. Heck, I'm supposed to be his ONLY! He's supposed to love me, *not some*— His thought was interrupted by the sight of Odie's rubber ball, sitting in front of him on the floor. —*not some stupid, sniveling, smelly, butt-sniffing DOG!* Garfield gathered his strength and kicked the ball with everything he had.

It wasn't the best decision he had made all day. He watched in stunned silence as the ball struck a floor lamp, which *CRASHED!* onto the desk. Office supplies flew everywhere, sending a round glass paperweight to the floor. It rolled at top speed, cracking into the entertainment center. The loudspeakers fell from their hooks and tumbled to the floor, where one landed—*SPROING!*—on an ornamental sword, flipping it into the air. In one clean arc it sliced through Jon's high-school diploma on the far wall, before it *SCHLEEKED!* to a halt amid the fireplace pokers. *PING!* A coal rake spun out and wedged behind the very bookcase before which Garfield sat, too dazed to move. The bookcase groaned and teetered. Garfield stared up at it, slack-jawed, certain that when it was all over he would have only eight lives left. He said his prayers, closed his eyes, and waited to get smashed to kitty bits.

Suddenly the creaking stopped. In the abrupt silence, Garfield peeled open one eye to see the bookcase suspended just above him, miraculously restrained by the stretched cord of a nearby lamp. He resumed breathing.

Whoops! He breathed too soon. To his horror, Garfield saw the plug slowly slipping from the outlet under the weight of too many books. He cursed Jon's recreational preferences one last time and wondered if there was lasagna in heaven. The last thing he saw, closing in with remarkable speed, was a hardcover copy of *Polka Hits, Milwaukee to Minsk.*

CRASH! THUD! (Meow.) Flutter, flutter, flutter.

There sat Garfield, unmoved and untouched, surrounded by books and shattered knickknacks. Through some miracle of modern science, the avalanche missed him by only a whisker.

His heart was still pounding when Jon and Odie skipped into the house a few moments later. Garfield looked at them sheepishly.

Hey, guys. How was the dog show?

Not long after the sun went down, the door of the Arbuckle home swung open. Jon emerged, hauling Garfield in his arms and looking very cross. He bent over and planted the cat firmly on the porch. Garfield tensed up and clung fast.

"I'm sorry, Garfield, but you leave me no choice." Jon's voice was obdurate and his eyebrows knit into a stern expression.

You can't do this, Jon. He's tearing me up. He's ruining

my life. You know me. I'm too lazy to just want to destroy your house. I was provoked. I was pushed, prodded, and driven mad. He summoned his most pathetic expression, which wasn't difficult, given how he felt. *You can't kick me out of my own house like I'm some kind of animal!*

"Good *night*, Garfield." Jon shook himself free, scowled harder, and stepped inside. He turned to see Garfield on his back with his paws in the air, international cat-speak for "I surrender."

This will teach him a lesson, Jon stewed, yanking the door behind him. The *SLAM!* launched Garfield skyward a couple of feet. As he fell to the porch, his heart fell with him.

Jon? Jon? You know I'm scared of the dark! JON?

Nothing but the sounds of crickets and distant dogs met Garfield's pleadings. He curled himself into a tight, fat ball and settled onto the porch, shivering from the chill air and the night noises.

A short while later, Garfield heard the sound of laughter filtered through the bathroom window. He uncoiled himself and sprang to the sill to investigate. There he saw Odie's collar and tags sitting on the counter, and Jon giving him a bubble bath in the tub.

How could this have happened to me? What does Jon need a dog for, anyway? I give so much more pet for the money. With me, you get nine lives for the price of one. I've easily mastered the physics of all sorts of helpful household chores such as opening the refrigerator, but Odie's so dumb his IQ test came back negative. Can Odie walk right foot, right foot, left foot, left foot? HA! Odie can barely walk, period. I offer one hundred distinct vocalizations to communicate with and amuse Jon, but the mutt can only cough up ten. Ever see Odie walk with his tail straight up in the air? NO! Only I, the domestic cat, can do this. What more does Jon want from me? Garfield broke into a morose little tune:

"*Used to have Jon to myself, day or night, there was no one else . . .*"

Jon pulled Odie from the tub and wrapped him in a thirsty towel. He hugged him and nuzzled his face. Now Odie wasn't the only one who had gotten a bath.

"*. . . From dawn till dusk, my meals would come, I'd lounge about, in my home . . .*
But now I'm out in the cold of night.
All alone 'til dawn's first light.
I'm in a new dog state of mind . . ."

Jon mopped his face and he and Odie left the bathroom. Garfield ran for the bedroom window, arriving in time to see Jon caressing Odie at the foot of the bed.

"*Used to think I had a home, a special place to call my own . . .*
But now the dog's in and I'm out.
I've got no Jon. I've got no clout . . ."

Jon crawled into bed and turned out the light. The digital clock radio glowed 9:30.

"*I'm in a new dog state of mind . . .*
I'm in a ne-e-e-ew dog state of mind!"

THE MOVIE

Garfield bowed his head, a cat defeated. A tear rolled down his furry cheek. Sighing heavily, he settled back onto the porch and fell into a restless sleep, dreaming of everything that had ever scared him. He dreamt that Luca caught him. He dreamt that he was being held prisoner on the distant planet Aerobics, a world without coffee. He dreamt that Papa Luigi declared bankruptcy and went out of business.

He was awakened by a scratching noise somewhere nearby. He opened his eyes to see Odie pawing the bedroom window and grinning at him through the fogged glass.

"Leave me alone," Garfield said, his voice flat. "You've won. You're inside playing 'humidifier' with Jon, and I'm out here all by myself." He turned his back on the window, walked to the top step of the porch, and looked listlessly into the cul-de-sac. His head dropped heavily to his chest.

The scratching stopped, and then silence. Garfield wiped away another tear. Next came the scraping sound of a latch turning, and suddenly Odie was sitting beside Garfield on the porch. He gently rested his snout on Garfield's shoulder and looked into his big yellow eyes with love.

"Odie, I can smell your breath from here."

Odie whimpered beseechingly.

"Odie, have you ever *smelled* your breath?"

The dog stuck out his tongue and licked Garfield on the whiskers.

"Don't take this the wrong way, but I strongly suggest you never do that again."

For one tender moment, Garfield remembered their earlier tumble throughout the house, and softened. "Still, you have some good points, not the least of which is your tendency toward blind admiration. If you agree to stay off the chair, walk five paces behind, and worship me as your king, we might be able to work something out."

Odie dropped a huge load of drool at the precise moment Garfield looked past his shoulder at the pet door swinging open on its hinges. In that nanosecond, Garfield saw the last few miserable days of his life flash through his head with stunning clarity. One day, everything was perfect. He had Jon to himself and all the television he needed to fill the hours between sleeping and eating. Then the next day, *woof!* Now he was defending the Sacred Chair, losing his rightful place in the car, and competing for Jon's attention.

With a speed reserved only for meals, Garfield dove through the flap and into the house, slamming the pet door behind him and locking it securely.

"Kick out the dog and bring in the cat!
Yakety yak, don't talk back!"

Odie sat on the porch, bumfuzzled. More relaxed than he had felt in days, Garfield trotted into Jon's bedroom, jumped onto his kitty bed, and snuggled up with his stuffed bear.

Hello, Pooky. Miss me? Pooky *had* missed Garfield, for that is what best friends are all about.

From their usual spot across the street, Arlene and Nermal observed a lonely Odie relentlessly clawing at the window.

"Can you *believe* what Garfield just did?" said Arlene, shaking her pretty silver head. "You *never* put the dog out at night!"

"Why not?" asked Nermal, watching Odie as he bounded to the door and resumed the pitiful scratching. Just then, a teenager on a bicycle rode past the Arbuckle house. Odie's single-mindedness was no match for his total lack of short-term memory, and his head whipped around toward the wheels with keen interest. He leapt from the porch and took off after the bike.

"Because," Arlene said, watching the chase disappear down the street, *"dogs run away."*

Odie joyfully followed the bicycle until it crossed paths with a pizza delivery boy zipping along on a moped. The dog abandoned the bike for the moped, running the traffic light between the cul-de-sac and the rest of The World. A bright red sports car caught Odie's attention, and now he turned and scrambled after the car.

The coupe zoomed down the busy street, with Odie following hot on its tires in pure doggy determination. The car plowed through an intersection just as the light changed, signaling "go" to a delivery truck on the cross street.

One side of the truck had a picture of Persnikitty and a box of Kibbly Kat. The other side sported a billboard depicting a giant bone and a sack of Diddly Dawg Meaty Chunks, which was all the inspiration Odie needed to change course yet again. He didn't know whether to chase the bone or the tires as he tore down ever busier avenues. The truck rumbled to a stop at the corner of State and Main and, gasping for breath, Odie pushed on—closer, closer, *closer* . . . until the light turned to green and the truck bolted forward.

The valiant little dog had given it all he had, but he was spent. The chase was over. Odie plopped himself down, panted heavily, and had a look around. Neon lights, storefronts, an endless stream of shiny wheels zooming in every direction—this was a strange new place, a world away from the cul-de-sac with which he had only just become acquainted. Odie cocked his head and stared at the frenzied activity and all the pretty colors, lost as lost could be.

Once he got his breath back, Odie slowly trotted the streets, nose down and ears forward, searching for home. He arrived at a church and lay down on the steps, shivering and drooling in the cool night air. He could see his breath and was momentarily transfixed by the vapor rising and disappearing right in front of him. Then he tried to think of what to do next, but because he was Odie, no thoughts came. He rested his head on his front paws and closed his eyes.

Suddenly, two human hands circled his belly. His eyes popped open and he looked up into the friendly face of Mrs. Baker, a stout woman topped with a mane of white curls.

"What have we here?" she said, concern lacing her voice. "No tags. You must be lost, poor thing. Well, maybe we can fix that." Odie licked her face and followed the woman down the steps and into her car. She chattered at a grateful Odie as they drove out of the business district and past neighborhoods that reminded him of the one he had left behind.

"Poor doggy," she crooned softly as she checked her rearview mirror and noticed Odie pacing in the backseat, looking out each of the windows in turn. "You must miss your family terribly, if you even *have* a family. It's hard to tell when you have no tags. But you're such a good dog, you're probably not a stray." Mrs. Baker flipped on the rear defogger for the first time since last winter. "Well, even if you are, it'll be no trouble finding a sweet pup like you a proper home. There's an excellent vet in town who is always ready to help place stray animals. If it turns out that you don't belong to anybody, Doc Wilson will fix you up with a nice new family lickety-split. That's how Mr. Baker and I got our Chuzzlewit."

She turned off the main road and onto a quiet side street. "Almost there," she said. "As soon as we get home, I'll make you a nice snack." Odie draped his head over the front seat and licked the side of her neck.

She pulled into the driveway, cut the engine, and opened the door. Odie scampered out of the car and followed her into the unfamiliar house. "Mr. Baker is away on business, and Chuzzlewit is probably sleeping somewhere. I'm afraid all I have to give you is some of what he eats. Even if it's not exactly right for you, I don't think a meal or two can do any harm," she prattled, filling a dish and setting it on the floor next to the water bowl. Odie dug in gratefully. Every now and then he stole a glance over his shoulder, until he remembered where he was and that his dinner was safe from Garfield.

After Odie finished eating, Mrs. Baker took out her camera and snapped a digital picture of him. She went upstairs to transfer the photograph to her computer and make a flier she would post around town in the morning. Odie continued to explore the lower level of the house, sniffing everything he came across and licking the things that smelled good. On the floor of the guest bedroom lay an enormous pale pink lump sleeping with a collar around its neck. Odie had never seen anything like this before. He approached cautiously, led by his olfactory nerve.

GROINK! EEYEEYEE! Chuzzlewit's eyes snapped open and he started to scream. Odie popped up into the air in fright and landed squarely on the pig's head. Chuzzlewit stood up and ran blind all over the house, his snout poking between Odie's hind legs. The dog clung to his back and howled. Because a pig can't see with a dog plastered to its face, it wasn't long before they ran smack into Mrs. Baker, who had come downstairs to see what the ruckus was about. Down she went, flat on her back and covered in pork. Chuzzlewit's sudden stop sent Odie flying across the room, where he bounced off the sofa and landed on the coffee table. He panted and drooled, his eyes riveted to the snorting maniac on top of the woman in the doorway.

Mrs. Baker shoved the pig off and slowly got up, rubbing her butt. "I see you've met Chuzzlewit," she groaned. "Maybe it's best that I keep you two separated. Come on, you." With one last angry (and possibly hungry) look at Odie, Chuzzlewit followed his master back to the guest room, plopped to the floor, and seethed. Mrs. Baker closed the door behind her and returned to the living room.

"Sorry about that, puppy. *We* love him, but he does lack social skills. Don't worry, you're safe now." She sat on the sofa, took Odie into her lap, and stroked his quivering head until he calmed down. It wasn't long before his eyes closed and his breathing deepened. Mrs. Baker slid herself gently from under the dog, patted him on the head, and went back upstairs to finish her work.

Odie fell into a happy dream in which he, Jon, Garfield, and Mrs. Baker gamboled together in a lush green meadow dotted with wildflowers. Every now and then, he let out a tiny, contented *woof* in his sleep.

The next morning, Mrs. Baker tiptoed past Odie, her purse stuffed with the DOG FOUND fliers she had stayed up printing late into the night.

THE MOVIE

* * *

A few miles away, and not quite so early, Garfield slept peacefully with his arms wrapped around Pooky. Sun poured through the windows, and the ginger cat stirred. When he finally pried his eyes open, he saw Jon, fully dressed and running like a girl through the bedroom. Garfield recalled his triumph of the night before with smug satisfaction.

Ahhh, morning. Beautiful, wonderful morning. Hey, Jon! How about we start the day with some scrambled eggs?

"Odie? Where are you, boy?" Jon darted from one end of the room to the other, looking under the bed, in the closet, and any other place he could think of. "Garfield, have you seen Odie??"

Maybe a small stack of flapjacks.

Jon ran from the bedroom to the back door and yanked it open. "Odie?" he cried, scanning the yard carefully.

Garfield patted Pooky on the head, jumped out of bed, and joined Jon at the back door.

Okay. Waffles, then.

Chapter Eight

Somewhere in the downtown business district, Happy Chapman stood on a pedestal, thinking and scowling. A small, wiry man with an enormous nose and a mouthful of straight pins fluttered around his customer, fitting the umpteenth safari suit of his long, dull career.

"A-we do-a something a leetle deefrent thees time, no?" chirped the tiny tailor, spitting pins. "Maybe a leetle flare here"—he yanked at the waist of the jacket—"or extra flaps here? *Bello!* Signore Imbroglione make-a you something a-special thees time." He patted Happy on his bottom.

"Flaps, flare, *whatever*," Happy said with distracted annoyance, waving the *signore* off with his hand. "I can't go on like this, Wendell. I need a dog."

"I think that's a lovely idea," replied Happy's assistant. "I know you've been lonely since the divorce, and I've *tried* to be a friend, but—"

Happy cut him off. "Not for me, you imbecile! For the act! If I could get my hands on a talented dog, wouldn't Walter J. just about *choke* on his Emmy!"

Wendell had been staring out the window of the shop, where his attention was now caught by a white flier fluttering in the breeze on a street lamp. "You mean a dog like Odie?" he said.

"Exactly!" Happy shot back. "He was great. Dopey-looking, spry, comfortable in crowds . . ."

"And *lost*," Wendell finished.

"And lost!" Happy said, not to be outdone. There was a beat, and then *"Huh?"*

Wendell pointed past the window at the poster, which bore the familiar goofy smile of the canine in question, under the words DOG FOUND.

The wicked grin that to Wendell always spelled "uh-oh" broke out across Happy Chapman's finally happy face. He got down off his pedestal and marched straight out of the tailor shop, pins and all, with Wendell following nervously behind.

"Hey, my safari suit! My masterpiece! My *flaps*!" the tailor cried, his European heritage a thing of the past. "You haven't paid me for that yet, ya crook! Get back here!"

By this time, Wendell and Happy had torn the flier from the lamppost and were jumping into the BE HAPPY–mobile. "I'll drive!" Chapman shouted. "You navigate! We have to get Odie before that idiot Arbuckle sees one of these signs!" Wendell looked out the passenger window into a hairy fist and just shrugged his shoulders at the babbling clothier. The Mercedes took off at full speed, leaving the furious little tailor to eat their happy dust.

Five wrong turns and a couple of stripped gears later, the car screeched to a halt in front of Mrs. Baker's house. "This is it!" Happy cried. "Five-two-nine-oh-three Euclid Street. Pull over!" The two men scrambled from the car and dashed up the front walk. Happy cleared his throat and smoothed his flaps, drawing a little blood in the process. He motioned to Wendell to ring the doorbell.

Mrs. Baker's pulse quickened when she saw one of her television idols standing at her front door, flier in hand. Odie and Chuzzlewit stood by her feet. Happy let loose his most dazzling smile.

"Hello there, beautiful lady!" he said, beaming, and doffed his pith helmet. "I believe you you've found my dog? He answers to 'Odie.' "

"O.D.?" Mrs. Baker asked, frowning slightly.

"*Oh*-die. It's a family name," Happy said, locking her gaze with his own. From the corner of his eye he spotted Odie drooling on Mrs. Baker's ankle. He stealthily slipped a hand into Wendell's pocket and pulled out a dog biscuit, waving it low so that only the dog could see. He hadn't, however, counted on the pig, who started to wheeze and poke at Happy's outstretched hand.

"Chuzzlewit, cut that out!" Mrs. Baker cried. "Leave the nice man alone. You know who he is, you've seen him on TV."

"C'mere, Odie," beckoned Happy, making sure that the aroma of biscuit wafted in Odie's direction. The dog's nose did not fail him, and in an instant he bounded cheerfully into Happy's waiting arms. Happy stuffed the treat into Odie's mouth and wrapped his hand around the dog's snout to muffle the crunching sounds. "*That's* my little Odie! Good boy!" He turned to the white-haired woman in the drab gray cardigan. "How can I ever repay you?" he asked, his voice dripping with sincerity.

Slightly overcome by this low brush with fame, the woman stammered with delight. "Why, an autograph would be splendid!" In her mind's eye, she was already taking down her husband's dusty bowling trophy to make room over the fireplace for this prize. The mah-jongg girls would be so envious.

"Splendid it shall be, then." Happy snapped his fingers at Wendell, who dutifully produced an eight-by-ten black-and-white glossy. Happy signaled to Mrs. Baker to turn around and bend over. Wendell rested the photo on her back and signed Happy's name to it.

Mrs. Baker took the photo and fanned her blushing cheeks with it a few times, looking at Happy with awe. Then she leaned in to say good-bye to Odie. "I'm sorry to see you go, little fella," she said, rubbing his dark brown ears affectionately. "I really enjoyed the night we had together. But you must be so relieved to see your master again."

Odie's long red tongue snaked from his mouth and slurped Mrs. Baker across the lips.

"Okay," Happy said quickly, glancing nervously over his shoulder to the street. "The fond farewells are over. Thanks for all your help, ma'am. Let's go, Odie. C'mon, Wendell." And with that, they all piled into the Mercedes and took off up the block, leaving a teary Mrs. Baker on the front porch with her snorting potbellied pig. "I'll look for you on television!" she shouted after them, waving a hankie.

"Time to get this show on the road," Happy said crisply as he cruised toward the city. "We've got a new act to work up."

A short while later, Happy, Wendell, and the new act arrived at the television studio. Persnikitty, who had been snoozing in his cage, jumped up and tensed the instant he smelled Odie enter the room. Happy sneezed as he pulled the frightened feline from the cage, popping straight pins all over the place.

"Get rid of the cat," he said, shoving him at Wendell.

"Get rid of Persnikitty?" Wendell was horrified.

GARFIELD

"You heard me," Happy snapped. "I never want to see this fleabag again! He's *hisss-tory*! And so are we. We're in the dog game now."

Wendell could not help but notice the dollar signs flashing in his boss's eyes. "Well, what should I do with him?" he asked sadly, stroking the poor tom's patchwork black-and-white head.

"I don't care!" Happy roared. "Do I have to think of *everything* around here? Take off his collar and dump him at the shelter."

Wendell winced but obediently left the studio with Persnikitty shaking under his arm.

Happy leaned over to have a good look at his new dog. "Wake up, America! And especially *you*, Walter J. Here comes *Happy* Chapman!" Odie was frightened by the sound of his voice and instinctively nipped at Happy's outstretched fingers.

"Ouch!" he yelped, raising his hand to threaten Odie. "So that's how it's going to be, eh? Well, listen up, you little mongrel. You work for *me* now." Happy grabbed Odie by the scruff of his neck and started dragging him toward the crate recently vacated by Persnikitty.

Odie planted his butt on the floor and sat with all of his might, but he was no match for the maniacal Happy, who picked the dog up and hurled him into the cage. He slammed the door shut with a deafening *greeech!* and scattered what remained of the tailor's pins in every direction, narrowly missing Odie's eyes. Odie winced and recoiled, a low growl escaping his throat.

"Try going to bed without *dinner* and see if you still want to bite the hand that feeds you!" Happy snarled, extremely self-satisfied with his clever play on words. He whacked the side of the cage once to drive his point home, crossed to the door, and let out another enormous sneeze.

Odie trembled and paced, terrified of his memories of a not-so-distant time when he lived in a cage, and frightened of a future he couldn't see. His scrawny tail was plastered fast between his legs.

Back in the cul-de-sac, Garfield was sunning himself on the porch when Jon burst through the front door, gripping a stack of "missing dog" posters. The round butterscotch cat watched lazily as Jon jumped into the car and sped up the block, out of sight. *I wonder if the anonymous tipster line at the department of motor vehicles offers a reward.* He yawned, warm and sleepy from the sunshine, and hoped Jon would remember to pick up some of that peppermint-swirl ice cream they both enjoyed so much.

Arlene and Nermal watched Jon's flight from their curbside seats, their heads together in quiet conversation. Garfield arose, stretched elegantly, and ambled over to his friends with the lazy swagger of a cat back on top where he belongs.

"Old Lady Haswell just took a pie out of the oven. Anybody interested?" Garfield flicked a tiny wink in Arlene's direction.

Arlene and Nermal eyed Garfield coldly, ears flattened. "Keep walking, creepo," hissed Nermal.

"Yeah," Arlene chimed in. Her tail was twitching, and not in a good way. "You don't deserve pie."

Garfield raised an eyebrow. "What's going on?"

"We know how much you hated Odie," Arlene sniffed. "We know how much you wanted him gone. It's been as plain as the whiskers on your face since the moment Jon brought him home."

Garfield was shocked. "Wait a minute! All I wanted was to sleep in my own bed. What's wrong with that?"

"And to do it," Arlene seethed, "*you cast Odie out into the cold, cruel world! For shame!*"

"We saw how you locked him outside last night," Nermal added indignantly. "We saw the whole sad affair from beginning to end. Odie never stood a chance."

"Now wait just one cotton-picking moment." Garfield shook his head in amazement. "I don't believe you guys! *I* didn't know he was going to run away. He's a dumb dog. You can't blame me for that."

"It's always 'I, I, I, me, me, me' with you, you, you," said the Siamese.

"Nermal, you're stuttering," observed Garfield.

"There's no room for anybody else in Garfield's world," Arlene growled, shooting Garfield a look that meant in no uncertain terms that their Saturday night date on the fence was now canceled.

"Any one of us could be next," Nermal added, with a knowing nod. He and Arlene turned their backs, uttered a final "*tsk, tsk,*" and stalked off down the block.

"That's not true!" Garfield shouted after them. "I care about a lot of things other than me. *I* care about *my* lasagna. *I* care about *my* catnip! I care about *my* bed and *my* house and *my* street!" Garfield realized that his audience was fading from earshot, and doubled his efforts. "*My* scratch post and *my* comfy chair! *I* really care about *my* comfy chair! So soft . . ." Garfield's eyes grew heavy and his voice trailed off, laced with a gentle rumbling purr. "So comfy . . ."

THE MOVIE

He drifted sleepily through the flaps of the pet door and sidled over to the lounger. On the way, he paused to take in the beautiful silence of the empty house. *Mine, all mine!* he thought happily, as he jumped onto the chair and stretched for the remote control. *The emperor is in residence once more.* He turned a few circles and kneaded, trying to get comfortable. No matter how he shifted his girth, the favorite chair somehow just didn't feel right today. On top of that, it reeked of Odie. *Might be time for some new slipcovers.* He settled in as best he could and snapped on the television, turning up the volume.

"Lassie's run away!" came the distraught voice of a young child. Garfield rolled his eyes and changed the channel. "Snoopy, come home!" wailed a little bald-headed kid in a zigzag sweater. *Click!* "Old Yeller! Where are you, boy?" sobbed a scrawny adolescent waving a shotgun. *Click!*

There was Snoop Dogg's new music video. *Click!* Onscreen, a dozen greyhounds lunged en masse, yelping and chasing a mechanical rabbit zipping along a monorail. An announcer's voice sliced through the loudspeakers. "Here comes Speeeeedy! The dogs are off and running!"

Garfield wiggled uneasily. *Five hundred channels and there's never anything to watch,* he crabbed to the empty house. *Click!* He turned off the television and fell into a restless sleep, hounded by dream fragments of crying little boys.

Some hours later, he awoke to the sound of Jon's frantic voice. He sat at the kitchen counter talking into the telephone, next to a stack of "missing dog" posters.

I wonder if Jon's too busy to fix me a snack.

". . . he's about fifteen pounds. Brownish-yellow with droopy ears. They're probably damp." The doorbell rang.

"Hold on," Jon told the caller. "Coming!" he shouted toward the door. "I'm offering a reward," he said into the phone, as he crossed the room to answer the bell. "He answers to the name of . . ." Jon swung the door open and almost dropped the telephone when he saw Liz standing there, smiling. He fumbled for the phone's off button.

"Hi, Jon," Liz said cheerfully.

"Wha-what are you doing here?" He gulped. A week ago he would never have believed it, but Liz was just about the *last* person he wanted to see right now.

"We're having dinner, remember?"

Garfield sat up. *Did somebody mention dinner?*

The recollection hit Jon like a sucker punch. "Right! Dinner! Of course. The two of us. Eating. Together," he stammered.

Two's nice, but three—three is more, and therefore, better.

Liz looked crushed. "You *forgot*?"

Garfield looked crushed, too. *How could you forget about a thing like dinner?*

Jon, who *had* forgotten, scrambled for an answer. "Of course not! I've just been, um, er, real *busy*! You know, deadlines." He tried to strike the pose of a man bearing up under Important Business Pressures, which made him look seasick more than anything else. "No, wait," he said somberly. His shoulders slumped. "I can't lie to you. I have a confession to make."

Garfield watched from the Sacred Chair and rolled his eyes. *Ladies and gentlemen, I give you the sweet nothings of that man about town, Jon Arbuckle!*

Liz looked at Jon expectantly and waited for him to get his voice back.

He took a long, deep breath. "Well, not really a confession. More of a declaration. I mean, kind of like an admission." He spoke haltingly, and beads of sweat were beginning to break out on his forehead.

Liz's eyes sparkled. "I love it when you do that."

"Do what?" Jon asked nervously.

"Trip over yourself. It's so cute!" she giggled.

Hang around here long enough, and you'll see him trip over himself so much you won't even notice it anymore.

"It's one of the reasons I had a crush on you in high school," she added shyly.

Jon froze. Even the sweat stopped where it was. "You had a crush on *me*?"

You had a crush on him? Nobody has *a crush on him. This is so boring. Could we get back to discussing dinner?*

"Yes," Liz said, smiling sweetly. "I thought you were really cute and decent and, oh, I don't know—not like those *other* jerks who would say just about anything to make time with me."

Jon's jaw was still hanging. "I don't believe this!"

Neither do I. Why waste time discussing the past when we could be on our way to the restaurant already?

"I had a crush on you, too!" Jon continued, shaking his head in wonder. "I mean, I was *so* into you in high school, but I thought I didn't stand a chance!"

"Isn't that funny . . ." Liz offered tentatively.

"Hilarious," Jon added.

I myself am rolling on the floor laughing. What do you say to Chinese?

After a moment of awkward silence, Liz asked "So, what's your confession, declaration, admission? Was that it?"

"Oh, um . . . uh . . . right," Jon stammered. "Well . . ." He couldn't do it. He couldn't bring himself to tell her about Odie. He didn't look Liz in the eye as he raced to the end of the sentence. "I did actually *forget about our dinner*."

Her voice fell a little. "Oh! It's okay. I mean, if you're busy, I can go . . ."

"But I'm happy you're here! And I wouldn't miss dinner for anything," he squeaked, forcing his voice to sound bright. "I can do my work later. Just give me a second to get my jacket." Jon ducked into the living room and saw Garfield sitting on the Sacred Chair. He paced back and forth, thinking aloud.

"What am I going to do, Garfield? I've waited my whole life for this night, but I can't go out with her and just *pretend* that Odie isn't lost!" He plucked his jacket from the sofa and absentmindedly wrung it between his hands. "Oh, Odie! *What* have I done?"

I've got two words for you, buddy-boy: "Plausible deniability."

"I've got to tell her," Jon moaned. And with one last fruitless peek under the sofa, he turned to leave the house. Garfield's eyes followed him to the front door.

Schmuck. Don't forget to bring home the leftovers and my fortune cookie.

Liz was waiting for Jon on the porch. She smiled warmly at him as he opened the door. Jon took a deep breath and turned to face her. "Liz, we can't go out tonight."

"Why not?" she asked, perplexed. So far, she thought the date had been going fairly well.

Jon summoned every ounce of courage he had in him. "Because Odie's run away," he said, in a very small voice. He looked off into the street, unable to meet Liz's beautiful raindrop eyes.

"*What?*" she gasped.

Jon died a thousand deaths. "He got out last night," he said morosely. "I feel just terrible about it. I've called the pound. I've put up posters. I've looked everywhere. I can't find him."

Liz extended a sympathetic hand and touched Jon gently on the arm. "Dogs run away all the time. Why didn't you just tell me?"

"I don't know," Jon said sadly. He looked at Liz for a long, silent moment. "I thought maybe he's the only reason that you're spending time with me."

"Come on," said Liz.

Jon lowered his eyes. "It's true . . ."

"No, I mean *come on.* Let's go look for him!" Liz tugged on Jon's sleeve and started to lead him toward the car.

Does this mean dinner's off? Garfield considered this conversation as Jon slammed the front door behind them. *Odie's run away. Jon's going to start crying like those boys on the television, lose the girl, cry some more, and . . . well, I've got this empty feeling. I wonder if there's any meat loaf left in the fridge.* With that, Garfield jumped down from his perch in the living room and padded into the kitchen to find out. He positioned himself on the counter, at the precise spot from which to make the leap and drag the refrigerator handle with his front paws on his gravitational trip to the floor. There was the sweet sound of the latch, and then a refreshing blast of cool air on his cheeks. Garfield peered inside and studied the selection.

Who says I'm not athletic? he purred, licking his lips. And then The Mighty Hunter chose his quarry and sprang, dragging a plastic bag of day-old meat loaf from the bottom shelf and onto the kitchen floor. Garfield tore hungrily into his kill, then stuck his head in the bag to lap up every last drop of sauce. He shoved the refrigerator door closed with his tail, licked his paws, and wiped his face clean.

He glanced in the general direction of the front door. *Make sure you have him home by midnight.* Large and back in charge, Garfield yawned and shook his head. *Time to do nothing.* He waddled to the bedroom and curled up with Pooky for an after-dinner nap.

Across the miles in the big city, Odie settled down into the pile of fur Persnikitty had left behind and sighed. He hung his head in sadness. A tear rolled down his cheek, joining the puddle of drool that had collected on the studio floor beneath his cage.

The next morning, Garfield sat in his chair watching television. Jon was in the kitchen talking on the telephone again, and the worry in his voice kept distracting the skittish cat from the surfer dude ripping a wave across the glowing screen. Garfield listened to Jon and could not shake the mental image of the brokenhearted bald-headed kid in the zigzag sweater.

Who can surf at a time like this? Garfield sighed and changed the channel, fidgeting uncomfortably where he sat. Christopher Mello appeared before him, standing with Happy Chapman. The safari suit was gone, replaced by the embroidered costume of a Swiss mountain climber: a velvet-collared coat with bright brass buttons, a red whip-stitched vest, a turquoise ascot, and a jaunty felt cap with a feather.

"This is Christopher Mello and we've got a special treat for you today, ladies and gentlemen! We're on location in

THE MOVIE

Happy Chapman's studio in the Telegraph Tower. What do you have for us today, Happy?"

Garfield regarded the screen dully. An oompah arrangement of "Edelweiss" drifted from the speakers.

"Why, thank you, Chris! I've been working with a very special new friend that I want you to meet!" Happy chortled. "Please give a warm welcome to Odieschnitzel!"

Odie hopped into the picture on his hind legs, wearing black lederhosen, the short suspended pants that made Bavaria famous, and a bright red vest that coordinated with Happy's. Garfield snapped to attention.

Oh, my! It's Odie! I found him! True, he seems to be living some sort of alternative lifestyle, but that's Odie, all right! And . . . I found him! Nobody but me, me, me!

"That's one talented dog!" Christopher Mello enthused to the camera as his head bobbed up and down with Odie's spirited dance.

"I'm glad you like him, Chris! Because Odieschnitzel and I have an announcement to make!" Happy grinned broadly, defying the words that came next. "Sadly, this is going to be my last show."

"It is?" stammered the host, clearly surprised by this turn of events.

"Yep. Ol' Happy Chapman and Odieschnitzel here are getting on the three o'clock New Amsterdam Limited tomorrow and taking our act to the Big Apple, where we've got an opportunity to be regulars on *Good Day, New York.*" Chapman's puffed-up chest strained the shiny brass chain linking the flaps of his jacket.

"This is news to *all* of us," said Mello, trying to recover his on-air composure, and hardly succeeding.

Happy beamed into the camera. "Well, it's been great

working on your little show," he said, emphasizing that last part a bit too much for the host's taste. "But your loss will be America's gain!"

Garfield was riveted to the television. *New York?! I've got to tell Jon!* He raced from the living room and burst into the kitchen, careening onto the stack of fliers at Jon's elbow.

"I'd like to raise the reward," Jon said into the telephone. Garfield pawed madly at his arm. "Two hundred dollars . . ."

Two hundred dollars?? Where does the fleabag come off being worth that kind of scratch? Do you know how much lasagna you can get for two hundred dollars?

Jon was quiet as he listened to the person on the other end of the line. "Yes . . . no . . . well, *maybe*." Garfield jumped into Jon's lap and let out a loud *"Meowlll!"*

Jon! Come quickly! Odie's on television in some kind of polyester pantsuit!

"Hold on," Jon said into the phone. He covered the receiver with his palm, looked at Garfield through half-closed eyes, and shoved him to the floor. "Not now, Garfield!" Jon returned to the caller and swept the exasperation from his voice. "No questions asked. Two hundred dollars."

"MEOWLL!" *No. No. He's there! On the TV! I found Odie! Jon?!*

"Garfield, not *now*!"

It has to be now! Come on! Garfield darted into the living room just as Christopher Mello was wrapping up.

"Good luck, Happy. Good luck, Odieschnitzel. Well, folks, that's our show. This is Christopher Mello signing off. Remember . . ."

"Be happy!" cried Happy Chapman, completing the routine for the last local time. Odie bounced up and down in

his lederhosen. Garfield paced excitedly, meowing vigorously at Jon, who strode in just after the show ended and cut to a commercial.

He looked at his twitching cat sourly. "Garfield, I'm really *not* in the mood for your highly unusual viewing habits." Angrily, he snapped off the television.

Jon! I know where he is! I could bring him back! Then everybody will know that I'm not the insensitive, self-involved, egomaniacal . . . Garfield caught a glimpse of himself in the mirror and stopped to admire the view. *Looking g-o-o-o-d!* he purred at his reflection.

Christopher Mello and his crew were packing to leave Happy's studio. "You could have given us some warning you were going to quit on the air," the host sniffed. "That was unprofessional."

"Oh, get over it. You're lucky I was ever on your stupid little show." Happy tossed his felt hat to Wendell.

"You're a real jerk, you know that?" Mello snapped.

Happy thumbed his nose. "Have fun on UHF!" he sang. Christopher Mello stomped out, his crew following with the equipment.

Happy grabbed Odie and shoved him into Wendell's waiting arms.

"Odie's not ready," Wendell said, worry creeping into his voice. "He's months of positive reinforcement away from performing consistently."

"I don't have months," Happy said firmly. "But I *do* have the solution." They went down the hall into Happy's private office. He unlocked a closet and pulled out a cardboard box. THE SHOCK COLLAR was emblazoned across the label.

"Happy!" Wendell said with alarm. "You promised you would never use that thing. That collar is inhumane!"

Wendell's words were lost on his boss. "That collar is this dog's future. You got a problem with that?" Chapman turned a menacing eye on his assistant. Wendell looked away without another word.

"That's better. Now, let's see how smart you really are," Chapman said, turning to Odie and dangling the collar just inches from his face. Odie whimpered and shook in his lederhosen.

Garfield was determined to get Jon's attention, but he was too busy gathering "missing dog" posters to notice what, for Garfield, was a highly energetic display.

Jon, you're wasting your time. He's at Happy Chapman's television studio, wherever that is. You can trust me on this. I saw him with my own eyes.

"Not now, Garfield," said Jon, distracted. "I've got to go out and keep looking for Odie." He left the house and closed the door behind him. Garfield heard the car start up in the driveway. Suddenly, he had an idea. He dashed from the living room to the kitchen and leapt onto the counter, where he got up on his hind legs and used a paw to nudge the cabinet door open. He searched and searched until he finally found what he was looking for, a box of Kibbly Kat food. He flipped the box over and, without pausing to even *consider* a snack, studied the colorful map on the back. It showed a photo of "Private First Klass Persnikitty," the patriotic costume choice of last year's audience poll, superimposed on a skyscraper surrounded by dozens of other office buildings. Garfield remembered what they always said on the television: *"Coming to you stee-raight from atop the Telegraph Tower . . ."* So, Persnikitty lived in the city, in a building with a really big point on it.

Garfield ran to the front door and squeezed through the pet flap in an effort to catch Jon before he pulled out, but no such luck. The car was gone.

The city? Garfield gulped. *How am I going to get to the city?* He went back into the house. It seemed emptier than it ever had before. *I can do this. I can go find Odie. I can leave the cushy comforts of home.* But before he did, he walked around the house and bid farewell to everything that ever mattered to him. *So long, Sacred Chair. Stay warm for me until I get back.* He went into the bedroom and jumped onto his special bed, rubbing it affectionately with his chin. *A nap would be so nice right now . . . but no!* He lifted his head, and his eyes met the questioning gaze of his stuffed bear. *Pooky?* Garfield purred deeply and gave the teddy bear a four-paw hug with a rolling finish. *Look after things and take messages while I'm gone, old friend. Don't be giving your pure heart to another.*

Garfield's next stop was the kitchen, where he rubbed back and forth against the refrigerator, stretching his hind legs rapturously at each turn. *And you? Don't even* think *about running while I'm gone. Before you know it, I'll be back to resume our relationship right where we left off. Tell me, are there more like you out in the world? I hope so. But if not, I will . . .* Garfield wavered for a moment, then continued with resolve. *I will . . . see you when Odie and I get back!*

He went to the living room and approached the television slowly, with a mixture of awe and dread. *Oh, magic box that is the source of all knowledge, respect, respect, respect. I kiss your ring.* Garfield stretched up on his hind legs and licked the dial. He hugged his body to the screen, soaking up the warmth that lingered after the morning's viewing. When he finally tore himself away, his coat stuck straight out and crackled with static electricity. *I am suffering from a small bout of separation anxiety, but it must be borne. Your devoted pupil is venturing out into the world to see if he has paid attention to your wisdom all of these years. I promise to do you proud.*

As the fur settled, Garfield moved on to the collection of framed pictures arranged on the end table. He gazed at a photo of himself with Jon, taken on their trip to Hawaii, right after the dynamic duo thwarted a tribe of volcano-worshipping beatniks and spared the island a fatal dose of hot lava. *As for you, Big Guy—I think I will miss you most of all.* A small tear trickled down the side of his velvet nose and onto a whisker, where it dangled for a moment before splashing to the floor. *We've had some good times, Jon. If . . . if . . . if I don't make it, never forget me, okay?* Garfield licked the picture and purred. *As if you ever could.* He knocked over the snapshots of Jon's family and nudged the "Garfield through the ages" photo wheel front and center.

A short while later, one frightened orange cat stood at the edge of the cul-de-sac, staring uncertainly into the great beyond. *Rules are made to be broken, right? I of all cats could host a twelve-part PBS self-help series on the topic.* Garfield worked hard to convince himself. *Beyond this intersection, the one I see almost every day during the milk hunt, is just another intersection (gulp) . . . and another (double-gulp) . . . and . . . I wonder if there's any more meat loaf in the fridge?* He turned back nervously, only to see Nermal, Luca, and Arlene looking sternly in his direction. In unison, they showed him their tails with a great flourish.

Garfield peeked out of the cul-de-sac once more and swallowed hard. *No! Now's not the time for a plate of meat loaf. Now's the time for a plate of courage.* With that, he lurched forward, spurred on by the six indignant eyes he felt watching his every move. A municipal bus passed by, belching exhaust and kicking up a storm of dusty debris that completely enveloped and choked the shaking orange cat. Garfield yakked up a hairball in the middle of the crosswalk, stepped over it, and ventured out onto the busy road.

The journey of nine lifetimes had begun.

Chapter Nine

The picture on the Kibbly Kat food box had included a smiling sun looming above the Telegraph Tower, beaming down on Private Persnikitty. Thus Garfield decided that it was in the direction of the sun he must travel. At first, he moved slowly, absorbing each new sight and sound with a mixture of curiosity and caution. A warm southwest breeze kept highly interesting objects, such as a tumbling leaf of nice, shiny tinfoil, in motion. Garfield stalked and pounced on his wind-borne prey until he was bored, and looked skyward to check his position. He was pleased to see that the sun was now quite a bit closer and stopped for a moment to admire his progress before pushing on with a more purposeful stride.

Some sights were familiar to him, places Garfield had spotted through the car window when he and Jon drove to the vet or the airport. He sidestepped puddles and paused occasionally to open his mouth and taste the air. After a while, he began to detect patterns in the growing activity. At corners, for example, he noticed that all the cars would stop when a traffic light turned red, and move when it changed to green. Yellow, alas, was unpredictable. At least this was information with which he could work. Garfield checked the sun's location once more and began to relax a little, now confidently continuing straight toward the fiery yellow ball.

He trotted down sidewalks and past stores, ignoring perfectly squishable spiders along the way. When he stopped at a corner to wait for the onslaught of cars and trucks to die down, his nose picked up the unmistakable blend of tomatoes, cheese, bread, and olive oil that screamed *pizza!* and his head swiveled hypnotically in the direction of temptation. There he saw a pimple-faced young man serving slices through a walk-up window. Inside the store, beyond the clerk, Garfield spied tray upon tray of rolls and pastries, facing what had to be the longest, tallest refrigerator anywhere on earth. What's more, *its door was glass,* and Garfield's jaw dropped as he took in the rows of cartons of milk, cream, and canned cheese spread glistening on the shelves. His pupils dilated with desire. He stopped in his tracks and marveled.

Who knew such a deity existed? We need to do a little home improvement as soon as possible.

Garfield's ears picked up a distant bark, reminding him why he was here. *No! I will not give in. I am strong. I am well fed. I have a mission. The pizza looms large, but the mission looms larger!* He glanced at the corner and the cars speeding past. *Still red. Still stop. Still time to see all the pretty food.* Garfield's paws barely touched the pavement as he drifted closer to the deli. He craned his neck to take in stacks of groceries piled high in the shop, and his eyes widened appreciatively at the sight of cereal, cookies, chips, and all manner of gastronomical wonder. So riveted was our hero that he felt the lean black tom, sitting sphinx-like in the doorway, before he saw or even smelled his presence. *Schwoomph!* Garfield smushed right into him.

"Beg your pardon," the tom said drily.

"Is this where you *live*?" Garfield asked, incredulous. Behind the cash register were no fewer than four of the ten greatest inventions ever, according to Garfield: doughnuts, a coffeemaker, a microwave, and pizza.

"Twenty-four/seven," came the reply. "What's it to you?"

"In there, with all the food?"

"Well, yeah," said the black cat. "So what?"

"So what? So *what*? You're sitting pretty in the world's biggest pantry, where the pizza is hot and keeps on coming, and you say 'So what?' Even *I* couldn't eat all of these cookies in one day, though I'd die trying."

The black cat's head turned to look back into the store. "This stuff? Who cares about this stuff? Leaves me cold."

Garfield detected the life-giving aroma of his favorite morning brew, noticed that the teenager behind the counter poured some into a cup anytime anyone asked him to, and needed a moment to recover from what he was hearing. Then he looked at the stranger suspiciously. "If it's not for the food, then what on earth are you doing here?"

"It's as good a job as any."

This was almost more than Garfield could comprehend. "Job? You *work*?"

"Of course I work! Everybody works. My whole family is in the deli business. Well, maybe not my half brother Nigel. He took a job at the Chinese restaurant up at the corner of Emily and Betty and nobody's seen him since."

Garfield noticed the blurry black-and-white moving images on the security monitor behind the cash register, and for the first time in his life seriously considered the prospect of employment. *Hey, we don't get that show at home. Premium channels, a bottomless coffeemaker, and infinite dessert right up front where it ought to be . . .*

"What kind of work do you do?" Garfield asked.

"You're not from around here, are you?" The tom had never met such a strange cat. "I'm a mouser, *duh*. Try to find a downtown grocery store without one. These humans all come in here and say things like 'Ohhh, look at the cute kitty! Here, kitty, kitty, kitty!' But do they ever stop to wonder what I'm doing here?" The black cat smiled slyly and ran his tongue over his lips. *"Idiots."*

I knew there had to be a catch. "Why would you chase mice when you could be clocking some serious sleep within earshot of the microwave that keeps on giving?" Garfield had seen something like this on television once, but had written it off as fiction.

"Why would I care about any of this stuff when this place keeps me in all the mice any cat could possibly want?" The black cat eyed the orange cat suspiciously. "What are you, one of those French exchange cats?"

Garfield took a few steps past the tom through the open door, pulled beyond his control by the bounty within. At once the black cat was up on his feet, his tail held high and quivering. A hiss started to develop in his throat.

"Waldo! No!" That nice young coffee steward behind the counter reached for a water pistol and leveled it in Waldo's direction. "What have I told you about spraying in the store? Bad kitty! Bad, bad kitty!" The clerk fired.

As water dripped from his whiskers, Waldo's ears flattened and he crouched on the floor. Through half-closed eyes he looked at Garfield and said, "This is *my* turf, basketball. Don't even *think* about making a break for the éclairs, or you'll be jockeying for position at the great litter box in the sky before you can say 'Kibbly Kat.' "

Kibbly Kat. Happy Chapman. Odie! Garfield backed down immediately, though not without a lingering glance at the pepperoni pie that had just emerged, glowing and hot, from the oven.

"Did you hear me, fatso? *Get lost!*" Waldo's tail flashed back and forth, and the low rumble in his throat grew louder.

"I think I already am," Garfield sighed. "I need to find the Telegraph Tower. I need to find Persnikitty."

Curiosity got the better of Waldo, who relaxed his stance a bit and cocked his head in confusion. "Persnikitty? Why?"

"He has my dog. Arlene won't talk to me. Jon's a wreck and about to lose the girl, risking the only shot at professional in-home spa treatments I'm ever likely to have. I've got to get the dog back."

"You have a dog?" Now it was Waldo's turn at disbelief. "And you want him *back*?"

Garfield's mind flashed back on the joyous day of dancing and tumbling with Odie. Then he remembered locking Odie out on the porch, and sleeping it off without a second thought. Next he saw Jon's worried face as he ran around the house looking for a dog that wasn't there, and felt very low indeed. "Even I can't believe it, but it's true."

The tom looked at Garfield for a long beat. "Well, you won't find Persnikitty here." He nodded toward the street. "The sun. Follow the sun. It will lead you to the Telegraph

Tower. You can't miss it. It's the only building with a really big point on top."

Garfield looked at Waldo with something almost approaching gratitude. "Small snack for the road?" he ventured.

"Beat it, sumo boy. This ain't your neck of the woods."

With one last look of longing past Waldo's shoulder, Garfield turned and slunk back toward the corner and crossed the street.

What a rube, Waldo thought to himself as he watched Garfield disappear into the throngs of human shoppers. *This town is going to eat him alive.*

The day was getting hotter. The wind had died down and heat rose in blistering waves from the sidewalk, blurring Garfield's vision. His eyes stung when he looked up to check the position of the sun. *Wow.* It was higher in the sky, but so much closer than it had been only a short while before— just about overhead, in fact. As Garfield slowed and panted from the heat, he clung fast to the thought that he must be getting close now.

At the next corner, he found himself looking down upon a miniature dachshund tethered to a short, skinny man in glasses.

"Arf!"

Garfield examined the dog coolly. "Hey. Don't I know you from somewhere?"

"Arf!"

The man glanced at his dog. "Thidwick! Leave the hideously large cat alone!" The man sipped his yogurt smoothie and tugged on the leash, but Thidwick stood his little patch of ground, defending it furiously.

"Arf! Arf! Arf! Arf! Arf!"

GARFIELD

Why is it that the smaller they are, the bigger their beef? "I just know I've seen you somewhere before," Garfield mused as he waited for the light to change.

Thidwick would not be ignored. With a force that belied his size, the tiny dachshund clamped his jaw firmly to the cat's tail. Garfield jumped in pain, dragging the securely attached little warrior with him. Now he remembered. *The Pan Ting dog show.* Down came the man at the other end of the leash, his face in the pavement and beverage splattering everywhere. Not one to pass up such an opportunity, Garfield leapt into the puddle, putting his tongue to efficient work on the yogurt while Thidwick held fast.

"Bet you were a *big* Pan Ting loser, Wicky, old boy." Garfield lapped up the last of the smoothie and looked behind him at the dog. "That's mine, and I want it back," Garfield said, yanking his tail from Thidwick's tiny jaws. He dashed across the street, leaving the dachshund with a mouthful of orange fur and the skinny guy scrambling on the asphalt. He stuck his tongue out at the dog and continued on his way.

Besting small, self-important dogs usually cheered Garfield right up, but as the blocks ticked past, the heat of the sun was beginning to get to him. The brief yogurt respite quickly lost all of its refreshment value. His pace slowed. His breathing grew ragged and hoarse. Garfield's throat was dry and his head ached. Before this, Garfield's idea of a long walk had been the distance from wherever he was in the cul-de-sac when Jon called to his food dish. Muscles he never even knew he had, which was most of them, throbbed with a shrieking pain that ensured Garfield would never again forget them. Tiny pebbles and thorns had embedded themselves in the soft pads of his feet, and there was a wad of bubble gum stuck to his front paw, oozing up between his toes. A ladybug flailed madly in the pink sticky mess. He tried to clean off the gum, and only succeeded in gluing his whiskers together. This made his nose twitch.

Garfield sighed and checked the blue sky once more. His heart fell when he discovered that he had *passed* the sun, and it was now behind him. He hadn't strayed from his route, he hadn't even gone very far, yet he somehow managed to overshoot his target. *Stupid sun can't cross the sky without a road map.*

Half senseless, he lay down in the shade of a sycamore tree and wondered what to do. The next thing he knew, he had nodded off and was dozing restlessly, dreaming about wondering what to do. He awoke a short while later to the blast of an eighteen-wheeler's horn, and knew what he had to do. *Follow the sun . . . follow the sun . . .* The problem was, the sun had done a U-turn and was now leading him back in the direction from which he had come.

I can't go on like this. I'm tired. Exhausted. Sticky, lost, and alone. I WANT MY TEDDY BEAR! I need strength. I need guidance. I need a sign.

Dully, Garfield noticed a large bus rumble past the curb where he had been sitting and wondering. Stretched across the side of the bus on a field of gleaming silver was the image of a sleek greyhound. *Dog!* This was the sign Garfield needed.

He watched as the bus pulled off the road and into a rest stop. The door opened, and out tumbled a group of grown men in matching burgundy blazers and large furry hats with tails, tittering like a bunch of teenage girls. One of the men hiccuped loudly, and this made them giggle even harder.

Some of them were hunched over in what appeared to be pain, jamming their knees together.

"Ohhhh," groaned the one in the suede buckskins. "Don't make me laugh."

One of the few upright gentlemen seemed to be in charge of all the others. "Listen up, brothers of the Fraternal Order of the Raccoon Lodge! Five minutes, everyone! Then we hit the road!"

"Boss?" came a slurred voice from a big fuzzy head in the crowd. "Rocky—*hic!*—made me laugh."

"This is our last stop before we get to the City Center! Whatever business you need to take care of, you'd better do it here. *Ziggy-zaggy, ziggy-zaggy! Zug! Zug! Zug!*"

"*Ziggy-zaggy, ziggy-zaggy! Zug! Zug! Zug!*" they all answered cheerfully, even those who weren't quite standing anymore. Everybody waved their arms in the secret brotherhood sign and then made a break for the men's room.

Garfield's ears perked up. *City Center? That works for me.* He hurried toward the restroom window and leapt onto the sill. He squeezed through the security bars and onto a supply shelf, carefully picking his way through the soft, fuzzy headgear the men had lined up next to the toilet paper. Garfield found an empty spot near the last hat on the end and quietly curled himself up next to it, tail to tail.

A water fight erupted among the Raccoons while they washed their hands. "Hey, Scott!" twittered the one they called Mark. "Heads up!" With a wicked grin, he lobbed a soaked tissue straight at Scott's nose, where it landed with a *splat*, bounced down the length of his jacket, and fell on top of the shiny bald head of Brother Jim, who was hunched over, tying his shoelace. This was quite possibly the funniest thing any of them had ever seen. The happy band stamped their feet and slapped each other on the back.

It may be that their purpose in life is to serve as a warning to others.

A loud voice cut through the hilarity from outside the bathroom door. "Okay, boys! Back on the bus! Look out, you big, bad city—here comes the Fraternal Order of the Raccoon Lodge! *Ziggy-zaggy, ziggy-zaggy! Zug! Zug! Zug!*" Screaming with glee, the brothers wiped their hands dry on their blazers and grabbed for their hats. They stumbled through the doorway, pushing and shoving and making merry like Christmas.

They lined up (sort of) to climb into the bus, a few of them weaving, all of them guffawing. Somebody burped. From a distance, the Raccoons looked like a garden of downy titian flowers lilting in the breeze. One brother in particular was weaving unsteadily and struggled to hold up his head.

"Ohhh," he groaned. "My hat feels like it weighs a ton."

Bite me, Raccoon Boy.

"Roy's wasted!" giggled Brother Scott. "It's not your hat, Roy, it's your big fat head!" The brothers sobbed with laughter and held on to each other so they wouldn't fall down, which one of them did anyway.

With a Cheshire-cat smile, Garfield flexed his claws and clung securely to Roy's hair, such as it was, as the man groped his way up the steps and into the bus. He stumbled down the aisle and fell headfirst into his seat, chuckling all the way.

Walk too much, twinkle toes? Maybe you should switch to pineapple juice.

Roy promptly fell asleep. His mouth drooped open and

he was snoring loudly. The bus rumbled out of the rest stop and hit the highway, with those who still could singing "I Burp as Much in Texas as I Did in Tennessee" at the tops of their lungs. Brother Mark took the solo. As the Greyhound sped down the road, Garfield peeked out the window, looking in vain for a mechanical rabbit on the guardrail.

Nobody, least of all Roy, noticed when Roy's "hat" quietly slipped off his head and dropped to the floor of the bus. Garfield picked his way under the seats, carefully sidestepping the boisterously tapping toes of the Fraternity of the Raccoon Lodge.

You left me back in Memphis, I was a sight to see!
You ran off with my brother, who ain't no kin to me!
I crawled into a bottle, and to Dallas I did flee!
Now I burp as much in Texas as I did in Tennessee!

"Everybody!" shouted Brother Mark. All of the Raccoons joined in.

Signed on at a dude ranch to forget and earn my bread
Worked real hard until a bull done kicked me in the
    head!
Since then beans is the only thing the cook will serve to
    meeeee—
Now I toot much more in Texas than I did in Tennessee!

As the crowd collapsed with hysterics and sound effects, Garfield started to notice the variety of luggage surrounding him on the floor. He lifted his head and put his keen kitty nose to work. Mostly he smelled crunchy socks, but he just *knew* there had to be a snack around here somewhere. One seat ahead of him, an open tote bag emitted the tantalizing aroma of peanut butter and jelly, mixed with bologna. Garfield caught a glint of plastic wrap poking out from the top. *Score!*

He crouched. *The Mighty Hunter spots his prey cornered deep in the abyss. "Aha! I've got you now!" he sneers.* Garfield crept quietly, closing in on the sandwich with all of the stealth inbred by thousands of years of previous cats. *The Mighty Hunter hovers above and looks the doomed quarry hard in the eye, letting him know his seconds are numbered. With one last sensuous drag of the tongue across his lips, the King of the Jungle lowers his head into the sinkhole and stretches his jaws wide . . .*

"Hey, Earl! How 'bout helping us out with that mouth harp of yours?"

Suddenly, two beefy pink hands dropped from above and started to rummage around in the tote bag. Garfield reared back just in time to avoid detection, his eyes glued to the sandwich as Earl pushed his belongings around the carryall in a woozy search for his harmonica. The sandwich disappeared deep into the bag and Garfield sat up abruptly, trying to keep it in his sights. *Wham!* He hit his head on the underside of the seat.

"Whoa!" roared Earl. "*Big* bump! Bus needs new shocks!" Nobody else had felt the bump, but his loyal brethren vigorously took up the auto-repair battle cry anyway. "New shocks! New shocks! Take it to the mechanic, hoist it on the blocks!" they giggled. Earl found the harmonica and slid it from the bag, scattering most of its contents around his size twelve feet. Somewhat dizzy, Garfield watched a ball of rubber bands bounce across the floor as he waited for his head to stop throbbing.

GARFIELD

Once the stars had cleared, Garfield's eyes focused on the sandwich carelessly lying at the man's feet. *A mere blow to the head cannot stop the Mighty Hunter. He pushes through the pain. Again he zeroes in on the helpless victim, now flushed from the cave and quivering at his fate. The warrior creeps. The warrior pounces.* Garfield landed on the sandwich and looked around quickly to make sure no more Raccoons were dropping from the sky. He spotted an empty expanse of floor and dragged the bag toward it with his teeth. Then he settled in, tore into the plastic, and took a moment to savor his kill.

Oh, magnificent peanut butter, jelly, and bologna sandwich. Yours is a noble sacrifice. You have given yourself over to a higher purpose, namely, fueling the search for poor Odie and restoring Jon's happiness. And that's enough of that.

Three or four bites later, the noble sacrifice was history. For the rest of the ride, Garfield tried to suck down the peanut butter lining the insides of his cheeks and pry his mouth open again. He had just about succeeded when he felt the bus slow and rumble to a stop. From somewhere above boomed the enthusiastic voice of the chief Raccoon.

"Okay, fellas! We're here! Buddy up and don't forget your belongings! *Ziggy-zaggy, ziggy-zaggy! Zug! Zug! Zug!*" One by one the Raccoons stumbled from the bus, giggling and punching each other playfully.

"The big city! *Ooooo!*"

"Just like I pictured it! Skyscrapers and everything!"

"Think they're ready for the likes of you, Brother Scott? Ha-ha-ha-ha-ha!"

"You doofus!"

THE MOVIE

Garfield listened to all of this from his cozy spot inside the bus, and rolled his eyes. *You can't make this stuff up.*

"Anybody seen my hat?" asked Brother Roy.

"Check the bus, Roy," answered the leader. "It didn't just *walk* away."

Sadly, Roy, it did just walk away. Garfield leapt daintily onto a seat and through an empty window on the driver's side. It was a long trip to the pavement from there, and he landed with a thud, but on all fours, of course.

He stopped to get his bearings. He saw a world to which the television had never done justice. What for Garfield had been wholly contained by a screen measuring thirty-two inches on the diagonal was now so big that it seemed to have no beginning and no end. He stared upward only to find that in the city, there was no sky. Well, hardly any. As he took his first tentative steps away from the bus station, the King of the Cul-de-Sac was feeling very small indeed.

Chapter Ten

Back in the snug two-bedroom house on the tiny plot in the snug little suburban community, Jon Arbuckle paced in the kitchen and spoke on the telephone. Deep lines of worry had carved themselves into his forehead. He walked from the freezer to the trash to the microwave, talking while he absently went about making lunch.

"No," he said to the gentleman on the other end of the line. "Odie's not a hound dog . . . Of course I'm sure . . ." His eyes widened as he listened. "No, I don't want *another* dog . . . Uh, thanks anyway." He hung up the receiver just as the bell sounded on the microwave.

"Garfield! Chow time! Come and get it while it's freshly zapped." Jon walked over to the counter and popped the oven door. Instead of bubbling hot lasagna, all he found inside was a soggy cardboard box with a *picture* of bubbling hot lasagna. Slapping himself on the forehead, he went to the trash and pulled out the frozen tray, put it into the oven, and tried again.

Where is that cat? "Garfield? C'mon, I made your favorite. Lasagna!" His call was greeted with perfect silence. Jon stared hypnotically through the glass at the plastic tray as it spun on the carousel. *Maybe he's just sleeping, for a change.*

"Garfield? Wake up!"

The quiet hung in the air like a shroud of fresh-fallen snow. A sense of dread began to sprout roots in Jon's gut. Garfield *always* woke up to eat. Jon sprinted to the bedroom and checked the royal bed, where only Pooky lay, resting comfortably and not talking, as usual. He looked under his own bed, but there was no sassy orange imp frolicking among the long-eared slippers and their matching dust bunnies. Jon ran to the den and searched the electric trains. Though Garfield could never have squeezed his way in, Jon checked the tunnels anyway.

Then he went to the living room and thoroughly explored the easy chair, which yielded no actual cat but was covered in enough ginger fur from which to fashion a brand-new one. Jon checked his work area, going behind the computer and into each basket and desk drawer. He kicked his way through the remnants of the enormous mess Garfield had made the previous afternoon, when that crazy cat had inexplicably taken down an entire bookcase.

From the corner of his eye, Jon noticed that something was not quite as it should be on the end table. Upon closer inspection, he saw that the pictures had been rearranged, with the photos of the family back on the farm cast aside and the flip wheel of "Garfield through the ages" front and center. He paused to look at a few and sighed nervously. *Ding!* The bell on the microwave went off. *That's it! Garfield slipped past me somehow and he's in the kitchen right now, watching the lasagna!*

"I'm coming," he called eagerly, as he ran through the doorway.

GARFIELD

One could have heard a pin drop. There was no fat cat fussing impatiently on the counter. Jon's shoulders slumped, but he meticulously went through every cabinet, pushing aside boxes, cans, and jars with rubbery arms. He opened the oven and the refrigerator, almost afraid to look. He checked the cookie jar, one of Garfield's favorite hiding places. But when he peered inside, all he found were a few macadamia nut cookies. No cat.

He must be outside somewhere! Jon dashed optimistically through the back door and scanned the yard. No bright orange patch to be seen anywhere among the greenery. Calling Garfield's name, he ran around the side of the house, stopping at the trash bins and rummaging through the garbage. No cat here, either. As he headed for the front porch, he was sweating with anxiety and roots of dread were snaking through his stomach. Somehow, Jon knew that his best friend of so many years just wasn't going to be in the front yard contentedly chewing the grass. His heart was beating rapidly, flushed with the adrenaline of fear.

"Garfield! Where are you, Garfield??" Jon shouted into the street.

Arlene and Nermal sat on the sidewalk and watched Jon with interest.

"You ain't gonna find him here," meowed Nermal. "The coward did the decent thing and ran away."

"Maybe he's trying to find Odie," Arlene offered hopefully. As angry as she was over Garfield's selfish behavior, deep down inside she had a soft spot for the big lug. Sure, there were other attractive toms in the cul-de-sac. Some were smarter than Garfield, or better hunters. Some were kinder. *All* of them had better physiques. Still, there was something irresistible about his confidence, courage, and straight-shooting style. And though she'd never admit it to anyone, she found his weekly variety act on the neighborhood stage downright charming. More than anything, she hoped Garfield was off somewhere making her proud.

Nermal sniffed. His blue eyes were icy. "Garfield, thinking about somebody *else*? Ha!"

Arlene looked at Nermal and replied with a heartbroken sigh. "Yeah, you're right," she said, resigned. "The coward ran away." She turned her head so that Nermal wouldn't notice the disappointment gathering in her beautiful yellow-green eyes.

In the city, tall buildings loomed over narrow streets, blocking the sun and casting menacing shadows. Cars inched along, bumper to bumper, blasting their horns with cosmopolitan impatience. On the sidewalks, people hurried in every direction, pushing past each other and out into the crosswalks with little regard for traffic signals or oncoming vehicles. They had important places to go, people to see, and things to do, and a small matter such as an approaching truck was not going to stop them.

Nobody noticed the fat, furry blob underfoot, carefully picking its way through the onslaught of human nature. Or if they did, they assumed it was just another bright plastic shopping bag that had puffed up with air and was tumbling through the streets.

The city isn't so bad, Garfield thought, fighting his way through the crowd and trying hard to convince himself. *It has its plusses. Art. Museums. Culture. Food remnants carelessly strewn all over the streets.* Just as he reached the other side of the road, a large cowboy boot loomed overhead, and Garfield stepped up the speed to avoid being squashed. He dashed for a nearby alley and sat for a moment to catch his breath, his heart racing.

In the spooky darkness he saw dozens of pairs of glowing eyes, all fixed on him. *Art . . . culture . . . and . . . hello? RATS! Rats the size of . . . RATS! Ha ha ha ha.* Garfield forgot all about the culture as the eyes circled closer. His tail began to switch nervously. This wasn't right. According to the laws of the food chain, rodents were supposed to be afraid of Garfield, not the other way around. Still, he could not ignore the fear mounting in his gut. Now would be an excellent time for some strategy.

"Why am I being surrounded?" Garfield asked aloud, going for a combination of casual and sincere while he desperately scanned the alley for a way out. "Some of my best friends are vermin, just like you."

He plastered on his most winning smile and spoke in an easy voice. "I've always been quite fond of rats, actually. You're resourceful, intelligent, and you can't beat that fertility rate, can you? Tiny little pillars of the community, that's what *you* are." Garfield took in the crowd admiringly.

A particularly large rat with very long lashes stood on her hind legs and waved her front paws in the air. "Come on, kids! Line up! Dinner is served."

The smile slid from Garfield's face and he swallowed hard.

"Yay! Yippee!" A dozen smaller rats still in their "cute" stage giggled and shoved their way into a ragged strip of energy, reminding Garfield a lot of the Brotherhood of the Raccoon Lodge trying to get back on the bus.

One little rat planted himself firmly on the pavement and crossed his arms. "I don't want cat," he said flatly. His whiskers quivered as he stared defiantly at his mother.

"You'll have cat and you'll *like* it!" snapped his father,

who was nearly a foot long if he was an inch. "Me? I'm starvin' for some meat over here." He moved in toward the blurry orange lump, letting his keen nose make up for the lousy vision that was the curse of the species. The entire family pressed closer.

Garfield backed up and tried to sound unconcerned. "Me? No. It's not meat. They measured. Under all of this gorgeous glossy fur, I'm one hundred percent body fat. Saturated, very bad for the arteries. No nutritional value whatsoever. Your cholesterol and blood pressure would shoot through the roof."

There was a beat as the rats cocked their heads blankly. Then everyone was talking at once.

"Body fat's good with me," declared the daddy rat.

"Mom, I've got dibs on his ribs!" shouted one boisterous toddler, salivating as he approached.

"Mom, I want cat and cheese!"

"Me first, Mom! Me first!"

"You always eat first! He always eats first. I want a thigh!"

Garfield was pretty sure he was turning to liquid.

"Quiet now, children! Quiet!" The mother turned toward their father. "Harold? Say grace."

"Yes, dear." The largest rat bowed his head. His bride and twelve little pups imitated him piously. "Thank you, Lord, for the bountiful, plump puss on which we are about to gnaw."

"Amen!" the rats cried in holy unison.

"Hey!" Garfield replied indignantly. "You're making a big mistake."

"Eating that roadkill on Avenue B was a big mistake," observed the matriarch. "You? You're a soufflé."

The rats started to creep closer, backing Garfield up

135

against a brick wall. Quick glances in all directions told the doomed cat there was nowhere to go. He was trapped, and about to become dinner.

"Now stand back, kids, while Daddy carves!" The large male flexed his front claws menacingly in the general direction of the orange puff. Garfield crouched and flattened his ears. His tail switched violently, slapping the wall. A loud hiss developed in his throat and he shook with fear. His whole life flashed before him, from his humble beginnings in the cozy kitchen of an Italian restaurant, through the happy, well-fed years with Jon, and even including the last few days with Odie, who was, at least, better than vermin. Garfield squeezed his eyes shut and nearly fainted from terror.

" 'Scuse me! 'Scuse me! Comin' through." A rat broke from the skittish throng and pushed his way to the front. Something about that voice was familiar. Cautiously, slowly, Garfield opened one eye. He saw that the speaker wasn't a rat at all. He could hardly believe his eyes as he watched Louis, the mouse from the cul-de-sac, emerge from the rambunctious rat family.

"What's going on here? Hey, back off!" groused Louis, nosing three baby rats off to the side. "Garfield! What are *you* doing here??" It was hard to tell who was more surprised, the cat or the mouse.

"Besides missing the litter box by a long shot, you mean?" Garfield collected himself and continued, "It's a long story, Louis. Jon got a dog. Yada-yada-yada. Then the dog ran away to the big city, yada-yada-yada, and I'm going to find him and bring him home."

Louis glanced at the posse of salivating, fat-happy rats. "Well, seems like you got yourself in a jam," he said coolly.

"Wish there were something I could do to help you out. Really, I do." Louis casually examined the tip of his tail.

The rats advanced. Garfield saw dozens of beady little eyes surrounded by wicked smiles. He could have sworn they were all chanting, "Yada-yada-yada." Fear surged inside of him.

"Louis! I think you and I still have an account. Remember— macadamia nut cookies . . . ?" Garfield hoped his delivery sounded delicious.

Louis thought about this for a moment. He really was quite fond of macadamia nut cookies, and the Arbuckle house was the only stop on his route that had them since the Polynesian joint on Solwyn Avenue went out of business. His mind made up, he turned to the snarling rabble. "Sorry, rat pack. This cat's with me."

A dozen rat pups squealed their disappointment.

"Move along, now." Louis shooed the family toward the street.

The mother rat knew when to cut her losses. "Who wants to go to the Red Lobster alley?" she cried enthusiastically to her brood.

"Yay!"

"All you can eat!"

"Seafood makes me break out."

"Restaurant food! Let's go!"

"Do they have Nemo?"

Garfield let out a long, relieved breath. "Hey, maybe next time, guys. Keep the faith. All the best with that rabies thing."

"Don't push your luck, fat cat," the daddy rat sneered from the darkness. With that, the family skittered away, looking for their next meal. Louis and Garfield sat facing each other in the spooky alley.

"What on earth are you doing in the city, Garfield?" marveled Louis. "You've never left the cul-de-sac in your life, unless Jon took you for a ride in the car."

"Oddly enough, all of my troubles began the *last* time Jon took me for a ride in the car. But that story will have to wait for later. I've got to get to the Telegraph Tower." Garfield's voice was urgent. "That's where I'll find the dog."

"Will wonders never cease?" Louis slapped himself on the forehead. "I thought I'd seen it all by now, but this is some kind of world when *Garfield* puts himself out for the sake of another. And a dog, at that. This I have to see. I can get you there. But we gotta go covert ops. Follow me, and pay attention."

Louis led Garfield down the alley to a pair of enormous metal Dumpsters overflowing with street bounty. The mouse skittered easily up a rusted corner and hopped into the pile of glorious trash.

"We need supplies. Get up here, Garfield."

Garfield stared up the six feet to the top edge of the Dumpster and the additional heap of garbage above. He shuddered. "I left my cleats at home."

"Never mind," called Louis. "I'll pass things down to you. Be prepared to catch."

Catch? Wouldn't that mean lifting my front paws? Garfield positioned the vast wall of his torso to deflect whatever Louis tossed over. As he turned, he saw hundreds of little eyes glittering through the darkness like stars in a blackened sky. His ears swiveled reflexively in the direction of their tiny murmurs, and what he heard made him wonder nervously for how long Louis's street cred was good.

THE MOVIE

Something unnatural about a friendship between a cat and a mouse . . . If rats could, I'd vomit . . . The cheese seems to have slipped off Louis's cracker . . . Too much time in the suburbs . . . Maybe the rabies have got him . . . Who cares if they're friends? It's not like we'd hesitate to eat any one of us . . .

Garfield gulped a tiny bit and yelled up to Louis, "Make it snappy, would you?"

"Hold your horses . . . Wait . . . I think I've found something . . . Here we go . . . *Fire one!*" Over the side sailed a hinged paper carton sticky with the memory of moo goo gai pan. It bounced lightly off Garfield's belly and landed face-up on the pavement in front of him.

"How thoughtful of you to provide snacks," observed Garfield gratefully, inhaling the bouquet with satisfaction. There wasn't much left but a few licks to tease his appetite. "What else is there to eat?"

"That's camouflage, country boy, not sustenance. Oh, I think I see something big enough for you. Stand by for launch."

As Garfield waited for his little pick-me-up, the shadow rats detected the aroma of Chinese takeout. Garfield tensed instinctively and backed up against the Dumpster as a dozen salivating rodents drew closer. Unaware of the drama unfolding on the ground, Louis grunted and strained to move the trash, and the sudden noises made Garfield jump. Meanwhile, the rats were now but an inch from Louis's yummy camouflage, and within striking distance of one very nervous feline.

"TIMBER-R-R-R!" came the shout from above, and a plastic mail bin plummeted from the sky, covering the terrified cat the way a lid sits on a butter dish. When Garfield opened his eyes to see what had happened, he found himself alone in a very dark, very small space.

The equally startled rats quit the paper carton and scattered for safety into the darker recesses of the alley. Louis scampered back down the side of the Dumpster and sat up on the asphalt, scanning the area for any signs of orange.

"Garfield? Garfield, where'd you go?"

"Meow?" came a small voice from under the mail carton. Then, a little stronger: "Get me out of this thing!"

Louis addressed the box. "Covert ops, remember? This is how we're gonna travel undetected. You sprint a few steps, then lift your lid to get your bearings, then sprint some more." Louis took his place under the moo goo gai pan. "Sprint, lift, sprint, lift. Follow me."

"Sounds like exercise to me."

"I can rejoin my buddies and you can go hunt this mutt on your own, if you like," Louis replied drily. "In fact, I'm beginning to think maybe I need *two* macadamia nut cookies . . ."

For all of his bravado, Garfield knew that without Louis's big-city expertise he might never find the Telegraph Tower. "One cookie, two cookies—*mi* cookies, *su* cookies," he said sheepishly.

"Then, let's go! Go! Go!" Louis cried. With that, one small Chinese takeout container scrabbled toward the street at the end of the alley, with a big white plastic box scraping right behind. Louis dashed across the busy road and gained the other side. He peeked out from his blind to see Garfield sitting and gawking in the middle of the avenue, his box propped up on his head.

The portly orange cat looked up with wonder. "The lights. The energy. So, this is the city? It's not so daunting."

THE MOVIE

"Garfield, hurry. That's no place to start sightseeing!" Louis called from the safety of the sidewalk.

"I'm going to make it after all!" Garfield shouted, giddy with newfound courage. He picked up the crushed lid from a Styrofoam cup, licked off the last drop of coffee, and flung it into the air just as the light changed. Suddenly, the mass of humanity that had been waiting patiently on the corner broke free and stampeded through the crosswalk. A seemingly endless tangle of legs, briefcases, and hand trucks swarmed past in all directions, knocking Garfield's camouflage clear and bouncing the astonished cat like a pinball.

Garfield held his breath and squeezed his eyes shut tight.

It was with the heaviest of hearts that Jon Arbuckle drove out of the cul-de-sac toward the vet's office. He turned on the radio to drown out his thoughts.

"You ain't nuthin' but a hound dog, crying all the time . . ." Jon sighed sadly and changed the station. "What's new, pussycat? Whoa-oh-oh-oh-ohhhh!" came the song stylings of Tom Jones. Whimpering, the distraught man twisted the dial once again. "I said something wrong, now I long for yesterday-ay-ay-ay . . ." Jon flipped off the radio in panic and despair.

Where could Garfield possibly be? The world outside of the neighborhood is no place for him to be alone. What am I going to do if I can't find him?? I can't imagine my life without Garfield. And Odie! A person couldn't ask for a better dog. How am I going to break this news to Liz? Just when we were beginning to get somewhere, I've got

*to admit to her that I can't be trusted to look after pets!
Now she'll never let me take care of her . . .*

Jon pulled into the small lot in front of the veterinary office just as Liz was coming out the front door. He jumped from the car and ran to meet her.

"Jon, what's wrong?" He loved the way her forehead crinkled slightly when her natural concern painted itself across her face. He only wished he hadn't been the one to cause it.

"I think Garfield's run away. First Odie, now Garfield," he said flatly. "I'm not exactly in line to be Pet Owner of the Month," he added ruefully.

Liz's eyes widened. "Jon, what's going on?"

He turned to face her. "I don't know, Liz, but you've got to help me. I can't find him anywhere. I can't live without Garfield. He's my . . . *best friend.*"

While Jon Arbuckle beat himself up for looking like a moron, Liz felt a flood of compassion for this sweet, sensitive man who clearly shared the deep love she felt for the animals to which she had dedicated her life. "Okay," she said softly. "Let's start in the park."

Chapter Eleven

As chaotic as the big city was, it still possessed a certain kind of order. The mass of humanity that had engulfed Garfield in the crosswalk eventually reached one curb or the other, and the dust settled into the lull. Louis peeked out from under a parked car to look for his traveling companion. Garfield was nowhere to be seen.

"Garfield? Garfield, where are you?" called Louis.

"*RRRRRowwrrrr?*"

Louis stretched instinctively toward the sound. Directly overhead was a blob of spiky, glowing fur the size of the sun, swinging from a street lamp.

"Garfield, get down from there!" Louis shouted crossly.

"No. I'm not coming down. I'm perfectly happy living out the rest of my life up here."

Louis sighed. "Listen to me, Garfield. We're friends, right?"

"I guess."

"Well, then, trust me," Louis said, stroking his chin thoughtfully. *It's going to take more than words to pry him from that pole. I need an incentive . . .*

Garfield rolled his eyes toward the sky. "Trust and friendship. This is the nightmare I find myself in." The view up here was a lot different from the sea of appendages on the ground. Garfield felt so small that he wondered why anyone had ever suggested that he needed to diet. "Louis, this is a gigantic city. How are we ever going to get to the Telegraph Tower?"

Luckily for all concerned, the ally Louis needed rolled into view. "Meals on wheels," the mouse said triumphantly, jerking his snout toward a perfectly round hot-dog vendor huffing and puffing his way toward Louis. "Hang in there, baby." The vendor braked to a stop on the corner.

"One, please!" came the crisp voice of a well-dressed man striding up to the cart. "Sauerkraut, mustard, and relish."

To Garfield's ears, it was the roll call of the angels. As the pleasure of anticipation flooded his body, his grip on the lamppost started to relax a bit.

"Okay," hissed Louis from below. "Remember, covert ops. Here's how it will go down. I'm going to create a distraction, get blubber boy's attention. That's when you're gonna drop into the hole at the top of his cart, see? Don't let go until his back is turned."

"Oh, and put some shredded cheese on that . . ." added the customer.

Garfield sighed dreamily and slipped a little farther.

The man paid for his meal and moved on down the street as the chubby vendor pocketed the sale. Louis looked up to see his friend now scrabbling to hold on to the lamppost, and sprang into action. He slammed himself up against the pyramid of soda cans atop the cart and then ducked quickly into the hot dog hole as the rotund little retailer spun in circles, sticky from exploding soda and not knowing which can to chase first.

Garfield fell from the sky.

THE MOVIE

PLOP! Splash.

"Ten-point-oh!" cried Louis, clapping his bony little rodent paws. "Right on target, and excellent form. Welcome to lunch."

The Olympic diving champ took in the rows of steaming franks and the variety of mouth-watering toppings. "Anybody hungry?" Garfield asked, taking a bite out of the nearest sausage.

"This is one thing we've always had in common, G." Louis laughed. "Pass the ketchup."

From above they heard the fat little man muttering and putting away the soda. *"Unlucky corner,"* he swore under his breath. He slammed the cart's lid shut, and suddenly Garfield and Louis were plunged into darkness.

"Ladies and gentlemen, the captain *has* indicated that we're ready for takeoff," said Louis in his perkiest voice. "Please buckle your seat belts and place your tray tables in their upright and locked position. We hope you enjoy your flight, and thank you for choosing Air Buffet as your carrier today." The wheels lurched forward and the boys felt the pavement rumble beneath them.

"This is riding in style," Garfield purred. "Sure beats the garbage heap."

"Mayonnaise."

"Mayonnaise," said Garfield. *This friendship thing can actually be quite pleasant on occasion,* he mused to himself, as he prodded white globs of fat toward Louis with his paw.

"So tell me about this dog," Louis started, daintily wiping his whiskers. "Translate the yada-yada-yada. This is new since the last time I saw you. Looks like a lot has happened in four days."

Garfield chewed his frank and was beginning to feel like his old self for the first time since he left the cul-de-sac. "All Jon's idea. The mutt showed up in the car one day after a trip to the vet. Goes by the name of Odie, though it's not entirely clear if he knows that. His IQ is so low it can't be tested—you have to dig for it." He took a swig of root beer and continued. "Good dancer, but nothing but cotton between the ears, and overly given to projectile drooling."

"He lives with you now?"

"Yes. That is, until, uh, the night he got locked out of the house somehow," Garfield replied, choosing his words carefully. "He's been lost ever since."

"So what do you care?" Louis asked suspiciously. "It's not like you've always wanted a dog or anything. Why not just let him go, and have your world all to yourself again?" Louis leaned forward and peered into Garfield's face. "You bump your head or something?"

"As a matter of fact I did, but that's not important right now," said Garfield, recalling his bus ride with the Raccoons. "It's Jon. He's tearing himself up inside over this. He might lose the girl. I need to get his life back to normal to keep the lasagna coming."

"So it *is* all about you." Louis sniffed. "I shoulda known. Same old Garfield."

"Well, Odie's not that bad . . ." the ample feline offered meekly.

"Do I detect a hint of mush?" Louis asked mischievously. "Could there be some actual softness under all those acres of flab and fur?"

Garfield stiffened a tiny bit. "Please. Odie is so stupid," he said drily, "he looks in the mirror and says, '*Who's that*?' But Jon needs him, and I understand stupid dogs can make excellent household help." He let out a loud, satisfied burp. "Life is like a giant hot-dog cart, Louis. You've got to be in it to win it."

The wheels screeched to a stop. Light flooded in as the vendor flipped open the food bin, ready for business. Louis peeked up to see the spire of their destination looming across the street.

"C'mon. Here we are. The Telegraph Tower."

They leapt through the hole just as the vendor was reaching in to dish up a dog. The poor pushcart man reeled back in shock and did the same circle dance he'd done with the soda cans. The animals scampered under the cart to avoid detection, and cast their gaze aloft.

"It looks much smaller on the box," Garfield mused.

"There's no truth in advertising," Louis replied cynically. "Well, I'll catch you later, Garfield. You're here now and I don't do skyscrapers. Good luck in your quest."

"Thanks, Louis."

"Hey," the mouse called back over his shoulder. "That's what friends are for. Don't forget—*covert ops.*" He skittered away and disappeared into the teeming city.

Garfield took in the building entrance, with its security guards, constantly revolving doors, and perpetual swarm of people. This kind of humanity had only gotten Garfield into trouble so far. He swallowed hard. *Why couldn't Odie have been dognapped by somebody in a town house?* He scanned the area, looking for a better way in. Off to the side he noticed five bright orange pylons surrounding a big gaping hole in the building. Two men in matching outfits with ACME AIR CONDITIONING SERVICE stitched across the breast pocket wrestled a large grate to the sidewalk and fussed importantly over gadgets.

This setup has potential. Garfield looked once more at the main entrance and the crazed people running in and out. His attention returned to the two men, who by contrast weren't moving much at all in front of the hole. *Definitely doable. What is it Louis kept saying? Oh, yes. Covert ops.* Garfield scurried across the street and ducked behind a municipal wastebasket, tracking the activity of the two engineers.

"So, Frank, how's the new baby?" said one of the men, wrangling with what looked like a television remote.

"Wet and noisy, Dan."

Sounds like Odie.

Frank yawned. "I get more sleep on this job than I get at home these days."

Dan squinted at his tool and said philosophically, "Yeah, they all come out of the box that way. It's a thing. She'll get over it in a few years, if you're lucky. Then you get a little time off and *boom!* She's a teenager and you think you're never going to sleep again." Dan fiddled with some buttons. "These readings look good to me. What do you think?" He thrust the gadget in front of Frank's face.

Garfield slinked forward and froze undetected among the hazard cones. He strained to maintain his position and wondered if maybe he should have ordered that "killer abs" video from the shopping network after all.

"Yep," said Frank. "I'll go inside and let mission control know." Frank walked to the main entrance and disappeared into the lobby while Dan continued with his diagnostics. The sixth orange pylon morphed back into a blob and flashed past Frank unseen. Garfield leapt into the hole in the side of the building.

He landed with a thud in a narrow passageway, the daylight of the street behind him and only murky darkness ahead. *Not another alley,* he groaned to himself. *They had rats in the last one.* He padded forward a few feet, until he hit a dead end. Directly overhead was an opening to the building's ventilation system, a steep climb of slick aluminum surrounding a boxy space barely wide enough for Garfield to fit in. He looked up into the endless void and sucked in his gut.

There's more than one way to skin this cat. I'm coming, Odie! And I'm bringing my A game! Garfield braced all four paws against the sheer metal walls, using the bubble gum on his soft pink pads for traction. With the great deal of effort made necessary by a lifetime of doughnuts and sleep, Garfield began to shimmy up the shaft one painful pound at a time.

Back on the ground, Frank made his way through the lobby and into a small room marked AIR CONDITIONING SERVICE CONTROL. Another man in the exact same outfit sat at a high-tech console, drinking coffee.

"Yo, Larry," said Frank.

"How ya doing, Frank?" Larry nodded at his colleague.

"I'm still on the payroll. Everything looks fine out there. How's the monitor?" They both leaned in for a better look at the schematic of complicated twists and turns that made up the building's inner climate control system. Larry pressed a finger to a green splotch in the middle of the picture. "Looks like we've got ourselves a blockage," he observed.

Frank nodded knowingly. "Hmm? Guess we'd better purge the system. Can I press the button this time? Please? Can I?" Frank's eyes sparkled eagerly.

"Frank, we've been through this. The union won't like it. Pressing the button is my job. It says so in the handbook."

"Aww, c'mon. You always get to press the button. What will it hurt, just this once? The union doesn't have to know."

As the two men argued, the orange version of the green splotch continued to strain up the duct, slowly rising higher and higher. *I've really got to start thinking about taking off those last eighteen pounds.*

Larry, per union rules, pressed the button.

CLUNK! WHOOSH!

Garfield stopped and looked down toward the source of the ominous noise.

Please tell me that was my stomach.

Garfield's fur began to flutter in the rising wind. The racket grew louder until . . .

Ah, blow it out your . . .

WHOOOOOSH!

Larry and Frank watched with Game Boy interest as the little green blob whizzed upward through the system.

A terrified Garfield was propelled like a rocket by the onslaught of cooled air. He smacked hard—*boing!*—into corners and ricocheted among the walls, pushed ever higher by the roaring wind. He soon got the hang of it, however, and began to enjoy the breeze at his back and the thrill of the ride.

Here comes the world-champion extreme snowboarder, up for his final run of the day's competition. The sky is clear, the air is crisp, and this is one slick course, ladies and gentlemen, not meant for lightweights. The champ surfs, cutting in and out of flags and over treacherous moguls, never even breaking a sweat. Woooo-hoooo!

In a corridor on a high floor, another Acme Air Conditioning Service technician puttered around a duct on which he was working. He had just finished screwing the grate back into place when he heard a strange squealing sound coming from the system, and he leaned his ear against the plate, trying to figure out what it was. The noise grew louder and louder until . . .

SPANG!

The startled technician was thrown back to the floor. He opened his eyes to see an impression newly molded into the metal. He couldn't be sure, but it looked very much like a ball with two pointy ears. This wasn't right. He backed away slowly, then turned and ran as fast as he could.

Garfield's abrupt stop at top speed put stars in his eyes. *I just got faced.*

Somewhere very nearby, a hot, sad little dog slumped in his cage and never even noticed when the air-conditioning whirred back to refreshing life.

After Garfield regained his balance, he crawled back into the darkness of the shaft, bulging its sides wherever he hit a narrow patch. The chilly breeze was drying his eyes out, and his nose had started to run. He remembered with longing the warm glow of the television set, now so very far in the past.

This friendship thing is way overrated.

He stopped occasionally to peer through the ceiling grates that separated him from the offices below. He saw people at computers, cartons of dry goods piled high, even a showroom full of racks of what they'd all be wearing next season, but no Odie. He pushed on, getting colder by the minute. *I'm an autumn. Blue is so not my color.* His teeth started to chatter. By the time he reached the last of the delivery grates, his body was shaking like an enormous mound of salmon aspic.

His jiggling girth was all it took to knock the weak screws

from the vent cover, and Garfield plummeted into the space below, landing on a moving box with a loud *thud!* He shook himself and had a look around. The big open space was piled high with cartons, but there was no mistaking the large green Kibbly Kat posters tossed into a corner of the room. This was Happy Chapman's studio!

"Odie?" Garfield hissed quietly. He couldn't see very far for all the piles, but his sense of smell told him Odie was around here somewhere. He quietly dropped to the floor and started exploring, softly calling Odie's name. From his vantage point so low to the ground, the heaps of corrugation might as well have been the skyscrapers of the city outside. Heavy black curtains hung from large pipes overhead, surrounded by all manner of stage lighting. Cameras and other equipment were scattered haphazardly about the studio.

"Where are you, Odie? It's me, Garfield." He picked his way cautiously around every corner, sniffing the floor and letting his nose guide him through the maze. *What's this?* He stopped suddenly, in front of a low plastic trough filled with sand. He craned his neck and sniffed delicately all around the perimeter, his whiskers pitched forward. *Smells like cat.* With an enormous sense of relief, he climbed into the box and lifted his tail. A big smile broke out across his face. When he was finished, he hopped out of the box and instinctively turned to bury his business, scattering sand all over the surrounding floor.

While he pawed methodically at the litter, his ears picked up a faint whining somewhere very close. He turned to see a large moving box over his right shoulder. The sound was definitely coming from there, and was now amplified with scratching. He bounded the step toward the noise, splooching a big, fat paw print into the small desert he'd created on the floor.

Garfield sat down, stared intently at the carton, and addressed the wall of cardboard. "Oh, Odie. I feel just terrible. Don't worry, I'll get you out of there." More whimpering, louder this time. "First I have to figure out *how*."

Splosh! Gurgle! Pant, pant, pant.

A seriously soggy Garfield looked overhead to see Odie's pink tongue, productive as ever, dangling listlessly from a metal cage propped up on the moving box. Garfield jumped back, shook himself dry, and noticed with horror his friend's droopy, frightened eyes. There was a strange apparatus dangling from his scrawny neck.

When Odie saw Garfield, he yipped and started to turn circles in the carrier, listless no more.

"Odie! This is so great! I found you!" Garfield chattered excitedly. "I'm so sorry I got you into this mess. Look, we kind of got off on the wrong paw. I mean, you can be *really annoying* sometimes. And you don't give me enough space. And you're a major-league suck-up."

Odie drooled happily at the welcome sight of his beloved friend.

"But," Garfield went on, "we have a common purpose. We share Jon. Jon needs us, and even more . . . I guess I kind of want you back home, also." The rotund ginger cat wondered what Arlene would say if she'd heard that. "So, stand back. Here I come!"

It was all the same to Odie. He was just overjoyed to see a familiar face, pure and simple, emphasis on the *simple*. He paced eagerly in his cage as Garfield leapt onto the table next to it and started to work the latch. He pulled on it with his teeth. He pushed at it with his paw. Odie contributed some lubrication.

"*I've . . . almost . . . got . . . it . . .*" Garfield gasped, tugging with all of his might, until *thwoing!* The lock sprung open and the door swung out, knocking the stunned copper cat back to the floor at the very moment Happy Chapman strode through the studio door, followed by Wendell. Garfield dove for cover behind a curtain.

"You think he's ready for the audition?" Wendell asked uncertainly.

"See for yourself," Happy chortled. He strode up to the cage and yanked Odie out by the collar, not even noticing that the door was already open. He pulled a small remote control from his blazer pocket, cleared his throat, and got into character.

"Wake up, New York! I think you're going to flip for Odie, 'cause Odie's *flipping* for you!" Happy winked impishly as his finger squeezed the trigger, sending a jolt of electricity through the shaking dog. Odie turned one somersault after another.

From behind the curtain, Garfield watched with his jaw hanging slack. *I don't believe this. I thought he was too stupid to do tricks.*

ZAP! Wincing with pain, Odie performed a series of backflips.

"Whaddya say to *that*?" Happy asked Wendell, with a wicked gleam in his eye. "This little shock collar was worth every penny I paid for it."

Wendell looked on with pursed lips and said nothing as Happy grabbed Odie and shoved him back in the carrier, slamming the door shut. "What time is our train?" he asked.

THE MOVIE

"In two hours," said Wendell, handing Happy the tickets.

From behind bars, Odie looked pleadingly in Garfield's direction. His body was quivering and his eyes screamed *"Help me!"* when Wendell lifted the carrier by its handle. Happy sneezed. The two men marched from the studio, and Odie's head trailed over his shoulder as his gaze remained fixed on Garfield's hiding place.

A plump furry head poked through the curtain and watched them go. *A shock collar?!? That's . . . that's inhumane! True, it's effective . . . and surprisingly affordable. But still. Odie faces a future of torture, neglect, and degradation. Nobody gets to mistreat my dog like that except* me. Inside, Garfield felt the passion of resolve gather and course through his kitty veins. *Now it's personal. Now it's time to . . . GET HAPPY!*

Chapter Twelve

Garfield waited a beat and then crossed to the door leading out of the studio. He cracked it open and stealthily poked his whiskers into the hallway just as Happy, Wendell, and Odie boarded the elevator. He needed an alternate route to the lobby, and fast! *The air-conditioning duct!* He looked back the way he had come, but knew there was no way he was simply going to float back up into the hole in the ceiling. He stepped into the corridor and had a look around. Something smelled . . . delicious.

Garfield trotted toward the bouquet, and found a tray of leftover food just outside of another studio door.

Oh, no. What should I do? Eat the food, save Odie. Eat the food, save Odie . . . When in doubt, multitask!

In one swift motion, Garfield inhaled muffin droppings, shoved the plate aside, and head-butted the tray to the door marked STAIRWAY. He body-slammed his way through, leapt onto the board, and flung himself onto the steps.

"Surf's up!" Garfield meowed. "Gravity, do your thing!"

He clattered down half a flight and whipped around the corner, picking up speed. Soon the breeze was blowing his whiskers back, and with every passing story the tray whooshed faster and faster. Around and around he went, careening out of control. A man who stepped into the stairwell on the third floor was knocked back by an indecipherable clay-colored blur.

In the lobby a moment later, the stairway door flew open and Garfield popped through as if shot from a cannon. He skimmed across the slick lobby floor as people jumped aside to avoid the streaking fireball. *Sweesh!* Garfield squeezed his eyes shut as he approached the revolving door at a dizzying speed. It captured him and then spit him out into the street, straight through the open back doors of a red and white delivery truck.

CRONCH! SPLUD! Rrrrrowr! Garfield opened his eyes to find himself covered with sauce, cheese, and noodles, and surrounded by an inordinate supply of Papa Luigi's lasagna. Boxes were piled floor to ceiling. Truly, this was the Promised Land.

Wipeout. Once again, my life has been saved by lasagna. Garfield swallowed an entire package in one experienced gulp. As he prepared to move on to seconds, he glanced outside the truck and saw Odie being carried away by Wendell, walking a few steps ahead of Happy. A cab pulled up to the curb and Wendell opened the door.

There they are! Nothing can stop me now! He turned to the lasagna with love in his eyes. *I have to leave now, but you could go to my house and wait for me.*

Garfield leapt from the truck and ran for the taxi. Just as he was closing in, he suddenly found himself entangled in a web of green string.

"Aha! No tags! I've got you now, ya stray!" boomed a voice from overhead. Garfield looked through the mesh and howled into the face of a tall, uniformed man with a serious-looking cap. "You're going for a ride. Into the cage with you!" the man said cheerfully, swinging the net. He slammed the door shut and walked around to the front of the vehicle.

Garfield peered through the bars of the animal control truck just as Wendell disappeared into the cab and pulled the door closed. The taxi took off.

No! No! No! This isn't happening!

"Is too happening," a voice snickered from behind.

Garfield wheeled around and stared right into the slathering jaw of the ugliest-looking mutt he'd ever seen, watching from a cage across the aisle. "What happened to your face?"

"Very funny, cat. Everyone's a comedian. Hardi-har-har," snarled the cur. "It just so happens I have a good personality."

"That's obvious. Where are we?" Garfield scanned the rest of the cages and saw an assortment of cats, dogs, and one ferret, all chattering among themselves.

"He nabbed me at the corner of Virginia and King," moaned a calico. "I was *this close* to ripping off a liverwurst sandwich, and *bang!* I'm in the truck."

"Pantywaist," a tiger stripe scratching nearby sneered. "A pro doesn't get caught for anything less than porterhouse."

"*Caught?*" Garfield asked nervously. "What for? Who caught us? Where are we going?"

The hideous mongrel smiled ruefully. "You'll see, cat."

Somebody get me out of here! Too many freaks, not enough circuses.

Eventually the truck pulled to a stop and then slowly backed up, beeping until it hit a loading dock. The doors to the cab were flung open, flooding the truck with light and revealing two uniformed men waiting with long poles.

"What have you got for us today, Deputy Hopkins?"

The driver rounded the truck and joined his colleagues

on the platform. "Just the usual," the deputy replied. "Let's get 'em transferred." They opened the cages and scooped out the animals with their nets, each carrying one at a time through a doorway and into a low-slung building. Garfield watched intently from the far corner of his cage, trying to figure a way out and back to Odie.

The deputy returned to the truck and approached Garfield with a gleam in his eye. *This will never do. I'd love to stay and visit, but I have a punch list today you would not believe.*

"Last but not least, here comes Sumo Cat!" The municipal employee seemed to enjoy his job just a little too much.

I am merely experiencing a cell surplus. You can never tell what kind of winter we're going to be in for this year.

WHOOSH!

Garfield found himself paws up, staring at the last bit of sky he would see for some time. He was dangling in a net at the end of a pole slung over the man's shoulder. *"Ooof!"* sputtered the man as Garfield swung like a pendulum and threw him off balance. They bounced across the loading dock. In another minute they entered a large room lined with rows of metal cages. Cats were on one side, dogs on the other, and everybody else was neatly stacked on the far short wall. Garfield recognized some of his recent traveling companions as the door slammed shut on his cell.

"Welcome to lockup," taunted the ugly dog.

"You don't understand," Garfield meowed after the man, who had gone to join his buddies for a cup of coffee. "There's been a terrible mistake! I'm trying to save a friend. I shouldn't be in here. I have an owner! Do you hear me? I AM NOT A STRAY!" The gallery of mangy cats began to snicker.

"That's what they all say." A pit bull named Spanky sat

GARFIELD

across the aisle and glared at Garfield. "Nobody in here is a stray. You see Clarence over there?" He motioned to a shaggy brown and white mutt who was slapping himself while talking to the wall. "Clarence swears there's a little girl that misses him. And him?" The pit bull nodded to a Siamese, sitting erect and lifeless, eyes straight ahead. "Crazy Red here thinks he's an Egyptian. Hey, Red! If you're an Egyptian, why don't you walk like one? Ha ha ha! It could just be me, fellas," Spanky cackled, "but I think something *sphinx* in here!" He threw his head back and howled with laughter.

"Yo, Spanky! Maybe Moby Dick here is telling the truth!" shouted a frowsy Newfoundland-Chihuahua mix. "Did you ever see a stray as fat as this one? Have you ever even seen a *cat* as fat as this one?"

Garfield turned to Spanky. "And what about you, smarty-pants? Are you a stray?"

"Me?" gasped Spanky. "I'm the victim of an acrimonious celebrity divorce. America's sweetheart, my big fat hairy butt," he added ruefully.

"That's all well and good," Garfield intoned drily, "but this has nothing to do with me. I really do have an owner. His name is Jon."

"They're all named 'John,' meatball."

"I *do* have an owner, and a home," Garfield replied hotly, "and if I ever get out of this hole I will never, ever, leave it again as long as I live."

Spanky had heard it all before. He rolled his eyes. "Cop a squat, stray. You're in the joint now, see? And unless your 'owner' "—Spanky could barely stifle a giggle—"comes to collect you, or some newbie tries to adopt you, you're going to meet the same fate as the rest of us. The big sleep." Spanky grew solemn and turned away.

"I enjoy a long nap every now and then," Garfield replied, brightening.

"I'm talking stepping things up from twenty-three hours a day to twenty-four, pinhead."

Garfield swallowed hard. "Hey, I like sleep as much as the next cat, but not permanently! GET ME OUT OF HERE!"

Jon and Liz threaded through the park on foot, calling Odie's name repeatedly. Dogs were scampering in every direction, chasing Frisbees and rolling in the grass, but there was no sign of the small tan mutt with the floppy brown ears. Defeated, Jon slumped onto a park bench as Liz continued to scan the open fields. Suddenly she shook Jon's shoulder and pointed to a lamppost at the end of the path.

"Look at that flier!" she said excitedly. "It says DOG FOUND!" They ran over to the light.

"Look, Liz, it's Odie!"

Liz jumped up and down and squealed. "That's great!"

A sense of relief flooded Jon for the first time in many a day. "Somebody found him! Five-two-nine-oh-three Euclid Street. That's just a few minutes from here. Let's go!" They dashed for the car and sped out of the parking lot.

"I know a shortcut! Turn left at this corner!" Liz urged. "Oh, Jon, I *told* you we would find him!"

"I couldn't have done it without your support, Liz." Jon sighed gratefully. "I hope he's okay. Poor little Odie, he was better off before he came to live with me . . ."

"Oh, Jon! You mustn't say such things!"

"I mustn't?"

"Of course not! This has been a crazy week full of un-usual circumstances, but Odie and Garfield couldn't *be* in better hands. And that's my *professional* opinion."

"Really?"

"Hey, I get paid to know what animals are thinking." She smiled. "Odie? Well, he doesn't think, but I'll bet he just went exploring and got lost because he doesn't really know his home yet. And Garfield? Maybe he's still getting used to the idea of sharing you with the new dog. I'd stake my prac-tice on it. He probably just went off to sulk for a day or two. But in all my years as a vet, I've never seen anyone who loves his pets as much as you do."

"There it is! Euclid Avenue!" Jon shouted. They turned the corner and screeched up to the curb, bounding out of the car and onto Mrs. Baker's front porch. Liz rang the bell as Jon shifted his weight impatiently from one foot to the other.

The tall gray-haired woman opened the door and smiled. "May I help you?" she said pleasantly.

"Hello, my name is Jon Arbuckle and I just found this flier that you put up for my dog, Odie."

Liz waved the poster excitedly.

Mrs. Baker looked at the paper and frowned. "I think you're mistaken . . ."

"I'm not," Jon insisted, pointing at the photo. "This is my dog."

"I don't think so," said Mrs. Baker. "That's Happy Chap-man's dog."

Jon was taken aback. "Happy Chapman?"

"You know, the rather large man with the cat on channel thirty-seven?" replied the woman. "He came and took Odie home just yesterday. Odie's a family name, you know. Such a nice man, that Mr. Chapman. Good day to you, and good luck finding *your* dog." Mrs. Baker smiled sweetly, turned back into the house, and slammed the door shut.

Jon's mind flashed on the memory of Chapman handing him a business card at the Pan Ting dog show. *"Happy Chapman doesn't lie. In fact, I'm always looking for a dog with Odie's unique abilities . . ."*

"Happy Chapman does *so* lie!" Jon shouted. "He took Odie! And how many cats have the talent to open a refrigerator? Do you think he's got Garfield, too?"

"I don't know," Liz answered quickly, "but we're going to find out! Let's go!"

The city pound had settled into an eerie white noise as dogs and cats snoozed fretfully or murmured in small groups. Garfield sat alone, wide awake and miserable.

I can't believe it. Me, Garfield, in the hoosegow. Oh, the humiliation.

"Hey, you!" Garfield called to a skinny calico in the cage above him. "How long will I have to stay here in the pound?"

"Until your owner comes to pick you up."

Jon doesn't even know I'm here. "What if he doesn't come?"

"Then it's curtains for you."

"I love climbing curtains!" Garfield exclaimed. "Do they also have screen doors?"

"You don't get it," the calico sneered. "This ain't no kitty amusement park. If your owner doesn't show, it's game over, pal."

Garfield had never felt worse.

"*Swing low, sweet chariot,*" he sang mournfully. "*Coming fo' to carry me ho-o-o-me . . .*"

"You couldn't carry a tune in a paper bag," said a feline voice from the cage next door. "Would you mind? You're bringing us all down." There was something rawther British about the way this cat spoke. British and . . . *familiar.*

"*Persnikitty?!?*" Garfield couldn't believe his eyes, but there was no mistaking the combination of accent and black-and-white patchwork fur. "What are *you* doing in here? You're Happy Chapman's cat."

Out of his colorful costumes, the former television star looked like a tired old man. "I *was* his cat, until I outlived my purpose. That scoundrel needed a dog, so he put me in this wretched place. Correction: The coward had his *assistant* do it. Imagine the ratings slide if the public caught Happy Chapman dumping his costar at the city pound." Persnikitty sighed dramatically. "All humans are the same."

"Not Jon, my owner," Garfield said defensively. "He's not like that. He only wants what's best for me. He feeds me and loves me and puts up with me."

"And it seems now he's going to *miss* you, too."

"But, Persnikitty . . ." Garfield wailed.

The weary actor cut him off. "STOP calling me that, okay? My name's not really Persnikitty. It's Sir Simon."

"Sir *Simon*?"

" 'Persnikitty' was just another one of Happy Chapman's acts of cruelty. He's stuffed full of them, he is," Sir Simon said bitterly. "I was trained in the theater, yet I'm destined to live out my days a broken-down stray. Oh, the indignity of it all. My talents were *wasted* on the likes of that slob."

"In an amazing coincidence, I'm trying to rescue the dog

that replaced you! Happy and Odie are getting on a train in less than two hours to become regulars on *Good Day, New York*. Which I wouldn't really call must-see TV, but hey, that's television."

Sir Simon sniffed. "That no-talent mutt is going to be on network TV while I rot in here? Who says irony is dead?"

"Wait a minute," said Spanky, from his cage across the aisle. "Did I just hear that right? You're a cat that's trying to rescue a *dog*?"

The whole place stopped dead in stunned silence. After a beat, the murmurs began again, more urgent this time. *Who ever heard of such a thing? . . . Must be something wrong with that cat . . . I hear too much fat can addle your brain . . .*

"I'm not fat, okay?? I'm just 'Santa-waisted'!" Garfield shouted, to no one in particular. He turned toward Sir Simon and pressed his case. "I know it goes against nature, but it's true. At first I thought Odie was a pain. But he's grown on me. Kind of like a wart that you want to have removed, but then you realize it defines you in some grotesque way."

Spanky snorted. "Have you been munching some funky Kibbly Kat? If so, know where I can get some?"

"None of you would understand," Garfield sighed sadly. "Odie is my . . . *friend*." He dropped his head into his paws. "Good God! What have I sunk to?" *I don't understand this myself. I wouldn't be in this mess if Odie hadn't shown up in the first place. It's all in the manual: Odie's supposed to chase me up trees and my job is to scratch his eyes out and humiliate him at every opportunity. I don't even recognize myself anymore.*

The door to the room swung open, and Deputy Hopkins strode in with an earnest little girl and her parents.

"What's going on?" Garfield asked nervously.

"Adoption," Spanky replied gruffly. "One of us is blowing this clambake."

"Here are the animals," chirped the deputy. "See anyone you like, Hannah?"

The child headed for the rows of cats, prompting a collective whimper from the canine side of the room. She walked up and down the aisle, studying each cage carefully. One cat was scrawnier and more pathetic-looking than the next. A skinny black cat had boogers hanging from his eyes. The tortoiseshell next to her was losing his fur in patches. The white and brown cat in the cage below was missing half an ear. Stray cat after stray cat, and Hannah couldn't find one she liked, until . . .

"There!" She pointed in Garfield's direction. "That one!"

Garfield jumped up and strutted back and forth in his cage, absorbing the moment with all of the restraint of Miss America. "She picked me! Me! ME! Not you, ME! See you later, saps."

Deputy Hopkins sprang the latch on Garfield's cage. He jumped to the floor and started to caress the little girl's blue denim overalls with his tail.

"Not this one," she said, stamping her foot. "THAT one. The one that looks like the cat on TV."

Garfield froze in his tracks and blanched as she pointed directly at Sir Simon.

That broken-down old bag of bones? You'd better have a large shoe box handy.

The deputy lifted Garfield from the floor, placed him back in the cage, and shut the door. Garfield plunked himself down, smarting from rejection. "Looks like they'll be calling you 'Persnikitty' again."

Sir Simon winked at the insulted ginger cat. "When I give the signal," he hissed, "run like the wind."

"What?" asked Garfield.

"You want to save your friend, don't you?"

"Well, yeah, but do I have to *run*?"

Hannah's father glanced at his watch with impatience, while her mother rooted through her bag, searching for a sucking candy. The deputy opened the cage, and Persnikitty jumped into the girl's open arms. She hugged him tightly, and the family turned and headed for the exit. Deputy Hopkins followed behind.

Sir Simon looked over her shoulder and made eye contact with Garfield. "Now!" he shouted. "GO SAVE YOUR FRIEND!" With that, the former television star leapt from the girl's grip and onto a lever by the door, using his weight to pull it downward. All of the cage doors slid open in one smooth motion. Cats, dogs, and even a stinky European domestic ferret bolted from their pens, making a break for the exit.

"*HEY!*" shouted the deputy. "Get back here!" He grabbed a net and started to give chase. The startled family ran through the open door.

"So long, sucker!" trilled Spanky with glee.

Sir Simon watched the animals spew off in every direction, and his eyes shone with excitement. "Once more into the breach, dear friends!" he cried. "Once more, and close up the wall with our English dead!"

Garfield inched out of his prison and gaped at the empty room. Tufts of fur floated by like just so much tumbleweed. Cage doors creaked on their tracks. "One more question,

Persnik—I mean, Sir Simon. How exactly do I *get* to the train station?"

The aristocratic feline looked at Garfield and broke into his famous grin, the one that said, "I just ate the canary." He leapt to the floor and motioned at Garfield to follow. "Okay, here's what you do . . ."

Chapter Thirteen

As the taxi pulled away from the Telegraph Tower, Happy threw his head back and let out a volcanic sneeze. Wendell reflexively raised his arm to cover his face and passed Happy a handkerchief. Odie lay in his cage on the seat between them with his head on his paws, oblivious to the fine cool mist settling on him from above. The shock collar around his neck crackled faintly from the shower.

"To the train station, please," Wendell instructed the driver.

Achoo!

Happy eyed his assistant suspiciously. "You got rid of that cat like I told you to, right? Triple-vacuumed the studio, sent your clothes to the dry cleaners, sent *my* clothes to the dry cleaners . . . *Achoo!*"

"Yes, boss, I did."

"Then what's this I see stuck to your pants?" Happy said, leaning over for a better look. He plucked at Wendell's slacks like a mother monkey grooming her young. "Aha!" Happy cried triumphantly. "This is cat hair!"

Wendell scanned Happy's attire and plucked right back at him. "So is *this*," he said hotly, leaning over Odie's cage and waving a spiky clump in Happy's face. "Furthermore, it's *orange*, which proves it did not come from Persnikitty."

Achoo! Happy wiped his nose and banged on the seat in front of him. "Driver!" he said crossly. "Can't you make this thing go any faster?"

The driver muttered something unprintable.

Happy turned to Wendell, whose attention was fixed on a scene unfolding in the street. A little girl of about four was standing on the corner, sobbing at the top of her lungs. Her mother, a pretty woman weighted down by the morning's shopping, tried hard to console her poor daughter as nosy passersby looked on.

"Emma! Sweetie! It was only a costume! The super-market does not have monsters, I promise."

Whaaaaa!

The young mother dropped her bundles and stooped to wrap her arms around the distraught child. "How about when we get home we watch the *Funny Bunny* video for the seventeen-hundredth time?" Emma began to calm a tiny bit. "That's right, and we'll have a tea party and invite all your stuffed animals . . ." The crying tapered off and Emma's shoulders relaxed in her mother's arms. "Good girl," she crooned. "And we'll have your favorite for lunch—frozen waffles."

WHAAAAAAA! Emma was ramrod-straight and back in full voice.

"Sweetie! What's the matter now?" cried the confused woman, looking into a scrunched-up face the shade of which could only be described as "tantrum red."

Emma gulped for air and tried to speak. "I . . . I . . . I like my waffles *toasted*!" She slammed the heel of her sneaker into the pavement and crossed her arms.

THE MOVIE

Wendell smiled to himself as the cab pulled forward in the heavy traffic. Happy sucked down an allergy pill. "Let us speak no more of cats," he said. "Snotty, walking allergens that just as soon pee in your shoe as scratch up the new sofa. They are a thing of the past."

Happy patted the top of Odie's cage. "You, my good man, are the future. Together we are going to take New York by storm, and then the country. Just *guess* who won't get an interview with Odieschnitzel, America's newest sensation!" Chapman looked at his assistant, irritated. "Well, come on, guess already!"

Wendell rolled his eyes. "Walter J. Chapman?" he asked mechanically.

"WALTER J. CHAPMAN, THAT'S WHO!" Happy jammed his thumb onto the remote control in his blazer pocket, and threw back his head and laughed when the sleeping dog popped up like a piece of whole wheat. "We should call you 'Toastie'!" Roaring with laughter, Chapman opened the cage door and removed the shock collar from the dog's neck. "You won't be needing this way up in the baggage compartment," he said, pocketing the collar.

Odie whimpered and shook for the rest of the trip.

The sun was bright on the pavement as the Chapman party pulled into the unloading zone at the train station. A friendly porter greeted their arrival, pushing an empty trolley.

"And where are we traveling today, sir?" asked the redcap, holding the door for Happy as he got out of the car. Wendell exited the other side, pulling Odie's cage behind him. "Oh! Mr. Chapman! I didn't recognize you at first! Me and the missus, we just love that Persnikitty. Got two of our own, bless them . . ."

GARFIELD

Happy waved him off with a growl. Wendell placed Odie on the trolley, where the chastened porter was piling the last of the boxes and suitcases from the trunk. "We're all set," the porter said. "Which train are you taking?"

"The New Amsterdam Limited to New York. Three o'clock," Wendell responded.

"Let's get this show on the road, shall we?" Happy snarled, striking off impatiently.

"One-way ticket, I hope," the redcap muttered under his breath. He and Wendell followed Happy into the terminal. The friendly porter turned to the assistant as they made their way through the crowded waiting room. "The Big Apple, eh? Ever been there?"

"No, I haven't," Wendell replied amiably. "I'm rather looking forward to it. I have a couple of cousins there that I haven't seen since I was a kid, Oliver and Holmes. I'm hoping they can show me around."

"Are you on vacation?"

"I wish!" Wendell sighed, glancing at Happy as they squeezed past the crowds at the ticket lines. "No, we're leaving here forever, taking our act to the big city. The boss has an audition tomorrow for *Good Day, New York*."

"Wow! Persnikitty in New York! Very sophisticated there. It'll be no more safari suits for *him*!" laughed the redcap, expertly steering the trolley around the endless rush of travelers and their things. "From now on, it's strictly black turtlenecks, an eyebrow piercing, and late nights catting around town. Where is he, anyway?" he chortled, surveying the belongings stacked high on the cart.

"He's, uh, *retired*," Wendell said quickly. "He'll be staying right here." *In a good home, I hope.*

"Retired! Won't you miss him terribly?"

"I'll cope, not mope," Wendell sighed.

"So what's the act going to be?" the porter asked, puzzled. He lowered his voice. "Chapman's *nothing* without Persnikitty." The cart wobbled, and a small piece of hand luggage bounced from the top of the pile and landed on the floor directly at Happy's feet.

Chapman wheeled on the friendly man, roaring. "Be careful with that! This isn't just luggage, you imbecile, it's my future!"

"S-s-sorry, Mr. Chapman," the porter stammered. He jumped to retrieve the bag and cautiously placed it back onto the trolley. It was then that he noticed the small, scruffy mutt curled up listlessly in the cage. He had never seen such sad eyes on a dog before.

All the porter could think was *This is your future?* but he didn't say so out loud. Instead he said, "Here we are—the New Amsterdam Limited. Take the bags you want to keep with you, and I'll stow the rest in the baggage car." Happy strode haughtily up the steps empty-handed and boarded the train while Wendell pulled their carry-on from the trolley. He tipped the man and waited for the claim checks. Before the cart and the man rushed away, Wendell leaned over and peered into Odie's cage. "I'll see you when we get to New York, little fella," he said softly. "Hang in there. I hear they have thousands of fire hydrants." Odie looked at Wendell mournfully, and the porter rolled off.

Garfield sat on a corner and reviewed the directions Sir Simon had given him. *Walk left to the end of the block and turn left. Check. At the next corner, cross to the other side of the street. Check. Admire self in reflective plate at base of lamppost. Check. What did he say to do next? Oh,*

*yes. Proceed one half block to the Nutty Nomad Hotel,
remember your covert ops, and hitch a ride to the train
station.*

Garfield looked down the sidewalk. Sure enough, straight
ahead was the telltale activity of people arriving and depart-
ing, plus all the employees who helped them do it. He had
seen this before, when he and Jon vacationed together in
Hawaii and Florida. Young uniformed bellhops hailed cabs
and moved suitcases with militaristic precision. Drivers
leapt to open trunks and hold doors for the passengers.
They all pocketed tips with a practiced sleight of hand.
Garfield trotted quickly down the block, slipping into the
occasional doorway to case the joint as he drew closer to
the hotel.

From his hiding place he spotted ashtrays, luggage carts,
and planters, all with the potential to provide the cover re-
quired by his evil plan. He evaluated his choices one by
one. *Too many stupid humans choking around the ashtrays . . . Those luggage carts keep moving . . . Aha! The
potted palm!* Garfield stepped out from the doorway and
crouched low to the ground, slinking forward like a Navy
SEAL. He slipped undetected behind the large stoneware
urn, pulled himself up on his hind legs, and peeked through
the foliage. Operation Curb Patrol was under way.

A stretch limousine pulled to a stop in front of the hotel.
The driver came round the side and opened the passenger
door, revealing a tall, slender woman in a large feathered
hat and a short studded leather skirt. Her sunglasses covered her face almost completely. She strode with a confi-
dent smile toward the revolving door as the flash of a dozen
cameras exploded under the building's canopy. Trotting
just ahead of her at the end of a hot-pink leash was a freak

of nature handicapped by a lousy haircut. The tiny white teacup poodle also wore sunglasses and black leather.

"Welcome to the Nutty Nomad!" chirped a well-pressed bellhop. "Do you have any luggage today?"

The elegant woman brushed past him without a word.

Each of the photographers tried to get the beauty queen to look his way. *Over here, Misty! . . . Miss Stutterheim! Smile for the camera! . . . Hey, doll, will you play Misty for me?*

The nervous little dog reared back every time a flash went off. Miss Ace Hardware bent over and scooped him up into her arms, showing the journalists her best side. "There, there, my precious little Rex-y Wex-y. You mustn't let the nasty paparazzi scare you. They're just bottom-feeders." She nuzzled her tousled white companion, who proceeded to lick the makeup off her chin.

The woman and her dog approached the planter that was concealing Garfield. Rex detected the feline scent and immediately began to yip furiously at the palm. He scrambled in vain to get loose from Misty's arms.

"Don't think I can't see you there, cat," yapped the feisty little dog.

"Listen, marshmallow boy, don't blow my cover," Garfield hissed.

"Do you know who I'm with? Do you know who I *am*?" shrieked Rex, nonplussed.

"I know exactly who you are if you don't pipe down," Garfield shot back. "First you're hors d'oeuvres, and then you're history." The tiny dog started to growl.

"Rexy! What's gotten into you? You're losing it over a *plant*. That's it, I'm taking you straight to the doggy shrink the minute we get back to Sheboygan. Shut *up* already."

GARFIELD

Miss Ace Hardware slipped into the revolving door, with Rex's head trailing over her shoulder and his hysterical barks fading into the crowded lobby. An earnest photographer on the move crashed into the glass wall abutting the door and slumped to the ground, his camera in pieces.

Misty's driver pulled away, and an empty limo pulled up to take its place in front of the valet. At that moment, an elderly couple emerged from the building. A bright, shiny bellhop appeared at their side, his hand outstretched. "Need a car, folks?" he said, tipping his cap.

"Yes, we do," replied the gray-haired gentleman. "How long will it take to get to the train station from here?"

Train station? Score! Garfield watched as the man's wife pointed out their belongings to the helpful young man. *That's the thing about cats: We're aloof, but we're clocking everything!* Garfield saw his opportunity in a small piece of unzipped hand luggage waiting to be loaded into the car. While the bellhop placed the larger suitcases in the trunk and the passengers slid into the backseat, Garfield dashed from behind the urn and dove into the open bag, quickly pulling the zipper closed with his teeth. He miscalculated, however, and his tail stuck out of the side of the tote. He quickly curled it around the bag, hoping no one would notice.

"This is the last of it," the young man called to the couple in the car, slamming the trunk closed. "Won't be but a sec now!" He returned to the luggage cart and grabbed for the tote, but was yanked back by its unexpected heft. Frowning, he gripped the straps with both hands and dragged the bag across the pavement. After he hoisted it onto the floor of the backseat, he had to stop for a moment to catch his breath. Then he shut the car door and leaned into the passenger window.

"That's some load you've got there," he gasped, extending his palm. The elderly man handed the bellhop a neatly folded dollar bill. *"(Pant, pant)* Yep, *s-o-o-o-me* load!" The traveler rolled his eyes and fished out another buck. "Thanks and enjoy your trip now, y'hear?" The bellhop banged twice on the roof of the car and the driver took off.

Garfield nestled into his bag and nibbled contentedly on a chocolate chip granola bar he found packed next to him. *Hitch a ride. Check!*

Jon's sporty blue four-door stopped just short of the curb in front of the Telegraph Tower. He and Liz jumped from the car and ran into the crowded lobby.

"We're looking for Happy Chapman!" Jon shouted to the security guard.

"The studio's on the eighteenth floor," replied the attendant as they sprinted past, "but I don't think he's . . ."

Liz and Jon were already in the elevator by this time, impatiently pounding the "door close" button. They rode up in nervous silence, tapping their feet absentmindedly and watching the lighted numbers tick by. When the door opened on their floor, they burst into the corridor like a river cresting its banks.

"This way!" Liz shouted, and they ran toward a large picture of the television star propped on an easel at the end of the hall. They pushed through the double doors and stopped, taking in the huge space.

"Odie!" Jon called. "Odie, where are you, boy?" He walked around the studio, scanning the stacks of cartons and technical equipment. "Odie!" The room was silent.

"He's not here, Jon," Liz said quietly, searching under the craft service table. "The place is deserted. Wherever Chapman went, he must have taken Odie with him."

Jon made his way over to Liz and hung his head in despair. "Now what are we going to do?" he said sadly, his eyes cast to the ground.

Liz rested a hand gently on Jon's sagging shoulder. "We'll think of something. Let's push on." She gave him a little nudge toward the exit.

"Garfield . . ." Jon babbled under his breath, standing stock-still with his eyes riveted to the studio floor.

"Listen, Jon," Liz said, her heart breaking. "Let's find Odie first, and then we can worry about Garfield. I'll bet he's smart enough to find his way home on his own, eventually."

"No, I mean *Garfield*! Look at that!" Jon pointed excitedly in the direction of his gaze, at a swath of sand piled up next to the litter box on the floor. "I'd know that paw print anywhere. He's been here!"

"Garfield?" Liz said, shaking her head in amazement.

"Either Garfield or Bigfoot, I'm certain of it."

Liz peered at the tracks in the kitty litter. "I see what you mean."

Together they stooped to study the prints and figure out where they headed.

"What are you two doing?" The security guard who had tried to stop them in the lobby loomed in the doorway. He had his hands on his hips and wore a stern expression of authority.

Liz and Jon jumped up at the sound of the booming voice.

"We're looking for Happy Chapman," said Jon.

"Well, you're not going to find him in that pile of sand," the guard replied. "I tried to tell you downstairs, you just

178

missed him! He's on his way to the train station. He's going to New York."

"Thanks, Officer!" Liz called brightly, grabbing Jon by the hand. They ran past the rent-a-cop, into the hallway, and onto the elevator. They were on the trail once more.

Garfield licked the last of the chocolate from the granola bar wrapper and tried to pull his exposed tail into the tote bag. *Privacy. Refreshments. This is what I call travel the way it oughta be.* Inch by inch, his tail joined the rest of him inside the sack, but not without leaving a flutter of paprika fur in the teeth of the zipper. Complete once more, Garfield settled in for a little nap as the limousine rumbled through the city streets. He awoke a short time later when he could feel the car slow to a stop and the passengers shifting in the seats above him. The back door swung open, and the elderly travelers creaked their way out of the car, assisted by an attentive driver in a snappy uniform.

"Oy, Murray. I think my arthritis is acting up," moaned the woman, rubbing her knee.

"Stop complaining already, Sylvia. You've done nothing but whine ever since we left the house," said her husband, who was feeling a bit peevish himself. "Now hurry up, or we'll miss our train." Murray swallowed antacid as he watched the driver unload their belongings from the trunk and onto a waiting trolley.

Sylvia turned to reach back into the car for her tote. She gripped the handle and pulled hard, but the bag wouldn't budge. She yanked again, with both hands this time, but still it wouldn't be moved. "My bag is so heavy . . ." she said, perplexed.

Murray started muttering in Yiddish and joined Sylvia in

the backseat. Together, they huffed and they puffed until they finally succeeded in dragging the dead weight out of the car and onto the pavement, where it landed with a dull thud.

"That's what you get for taking all the soap and shampoo," Murray said, through gritted teeth.

"But they put it in the room for you to take!" wailed Sylvia.

Nobody noticed when Garfield's tail started to slip back through the small hole where the bag was partially unzipped.

There was no room left on the cart, so Murray and Sylvia set about heaving the bag into the revolving door while the redcap wheeled through the sliders with the trolley. The couple strained awkwardly in the small pie-shaped space, moving the bag a few inches at a time, then stopping to rest with their hands pressed up against the glass. Other travelers began to pile up on either side, waiting for the door to spin free and allow them to pass. With each jerk on the bag, Garfield's tail popped through the opening just a little bit more, until it was completely exposed. He couldn't help it. The tail just wanted to go that way.

The couple were breathing hard. The glass was beginning to fog from their exertion. "Okay, Sylvia. I think one more good, hard tug and we'll be on the other side," gasped Murray. "Remember when you gave birth to Irving? It's just like that, only we pull, not push. Ready? One, two, three . . ."

Fwomp! They jerked forward and bounced into the station, expecting to be free of the door, but *ssschlupp!* Garfield's tail, now fully extended, was stuck between the door's rubber sweep and the edge of the rounded glass housing. The elderly couple jerked to a halt, landing on their butts. The impatient crowd outside the station pushed forward, and Garfield's tail sprang free. Murray and Sylvia slowly got up, moaned, and hoisted their load clear of the stampeding crowd.

"Murray," Sylvia croaked. "I can't go on. Please, just a little rest."

With that, they dropped the bag to the floor and Murray mopped his brow with a hankie. "I swear, Sylvia, you and your hotel freebies are going to be the death of me." Inside, Garfield pawed the zipper open and *sproing*ed out of the tote like a jack-in-the-box.

Hey! Ease up on the old bag!

The gray-haired couple looked on, astonished, as Garfield took off in a puff of fur, zigzagging through the feet and the luggage of the voyaging masses.

"Out of my way! I'm on a mission!" he cried, though all anyone could really make out was "Meow." "I've got to save my . . ."

SCREEEECH! Garfield skidded to a halt at the entrance to the Pasta Pomodoro restaurant, conveniently located on the main concourse, just across from the newsstand. The house specialties were proudly showcased on a table out front.

". . . lasagna!?!" This was a real pickle. *Lasagna . . . dog . . . lasagna . . . dog . . . Why, God? Why test me this way?* Garfield moaned, staring at the inviting layers of cheese and sauce congealing under the hot lights. *Blood sugar . . . low. But . . . MUST SAVE MY FRIEND!* He started to go, and then turned to look over his shoulder. "I'll be back," he assured the pasta dish.

A series of shrill beeps drew the cat's attention to a luggage tram rolling through the station. Garfield vaulted onto the pile of suitcases, wedged himself between a pair of knapsacks, and settled in for the free ride, never taking his eyes from the receding sight of Pasta Pomodoro.

At that very moment, Jon's car careened to a stop outside the station, and he and Liz leapt to the curb. A cop was on them immediately.

"Hey! You can't park here! The red zone is for loading and unloading *only*!" cried the officer, waving his hand.

"I have a veterinary emergency!" Liz shot back in her most professional voice, pulling a red leather wallet from her purse. She flipped it open and flashed a card at the policeman as they buzzed right past him with no thought of stopping. They spun through the revolving door, leaving the confused officer scratching his head and wondering whether a veterinary emergency qualified as an exception to the no-parking rules. There was a quota to meet. He decided to write a ticket anyway, just to be on the safe side.

"That was pretty impressive! What did you show him?" Jon asked admiringly, as they emerged inside the terminal. Liz grinned as she handed him her wallet. Her veterinary "ID card" was nothing more than a Kibbly Kat wallet calendar with a picture of a smiling Persnikitty in scuba gear. Jon laughed and said, "Well, now I'm *really* impressed!"

"Which way?" Liz wondered, as a tram passed in front of them, blocking their path. Neither of them noticed the flash of orange tail that swished between two backpacks.

"*Last call for the New Amsterdam Limited, express train to Grand Central Station, New York City!*" boomed a voice from the loudspeakers. "*Track eleven!*"

"This way!" cried Jon, pointing. They took off for the platform.

* * *

THE MOVIE

Happy and Wendell were settling at a table in the dining car just as the conductor called, "All aboard!" A smartly dressed steward approached the table with a towel folded neatly over one arm. "Welcome to the New Amsterdam Limited. What will you be having today, salmon, steak, or lasagna?"

"*Puh!* Steak, so rare that it's still mooing," Happy sneered. "I *hate* lasagna."

"And you, sir?" the waiter asked, turning to Wendell. "Raw steak as well?"

"No," Wendell said. "I'm rather attached to my arteries. I'll have the salmon. And a glass of iced tea."

The steward made notes on his pad. "Something to drink for you?" he inquired of Happy.

"Coffee. The strongest, blackest, hottest brew this bucket of bolts has to offer."

"Okay, gentlemen, I'll be right back with your salads."

"How long until we pull out of the station?" Happy asked grumpily.

"Oh, just another minute or two, sir."

Happy dove for the breadsticks.

Chapter Fourteen

Once it became apparent to Garfield that the luggage tram was more or less just riding around in circles, he disembarked and sat down to have himself a think. *I'm never going to find Odie this way. I need a plan. I need facts. I need a sign.*

Did somebody say "sign"? High on the nearest wall Garfield spied an enormous arrivals-departures board listing trains, times, and platforms. Directly below was a bank of two dozen monitors that showed activity all over the station. Garfield's huge golden eyes lit upon the flickering images.

Oh, magic box who is the source of all knowledge, and who in partnership with the refrigerator has helped to build a stronger, smarter Garfield twelve ways . . . I knew I could depend on you in my hour of need. You and several of your friends, apparently. Garfield scanned the live feeds one by one. *Tell me, wise ones—respect, respect— where is Odie right this minute?*

Something shiny caught Garfield's attention on the screen marked PLATFORM 11. He saw an overhead shot of two men seated at a small table set with a cloth and, *mmm*, a breadbasket. Light glanced off the head of the man whose

184

back was to the camera. *I've seen that bald spot some-where before!* Garfield's eyes took in the rest of the scene, and sitting across from billiard boy was Wendell, Happy Chapman's hapless assistant. Wendell appeared to be duck-ing as Happy menacingly waved a fork in the face of the young man setting the table. *He may be evil, but he travels first class. Lucky eleven, here I come!*

With more speed than Garfield had ever considered in his life, he tore like lightning from the waiting area and through the archway that led to the track. No one and noth-ing got in his way as he scrambled up the stairway to the platform, but there was a good reason for this. The area was deserted. As soon as he reached the top step, Garfield understood why his trip was unfettered by all those pesky humans and their confounded things. The New Amster-dam Limited was rolling away from the station, and it was taking Odie with it.

Garfield slumped, defeated. *Maybe if I'd been exercis-ing all these years I could have run faster. Maybe if I didn't eat that last granola bar, or the previous 27,375 snacks I've had in my life, I could have made it in time. And how many of those snacks do I remember, huh? What good are they to me now, when I cannot rescue my friend?* Garfield ruminated and stared for a beat. Across the track on Platform Ten he spotted a small boy walking hand in hand with his mother. Tucked under his free arm was a toy train.

Hey, if Jon can do it, how hard can it be? Rejuvenated by the sheer brilliance of his idea, Garfield shot back through the archway and into the station, right past the feet of Jon and Liz, who stood staring up at the information board. The New Amsterdam Limited was no longer listed.

GARFIELD

"Oh, no! We're too late," Liz cried.

Jon shook his head, unwilling to give up now. "There
must be *something* they can do to stop the train." He
tapped his finger against his left ear the way he always did
when he was deep in thought, and then turned to Liz and
grabbed her by the hands. "Come on! I have an idea!"

Off they ran, in precisely the opposite direction from
Garfield, who had just located *his* idea: the Master Switch
Panel Control Room. Fate continued to smile on the cat with
a mission, for at that very moment, an engineer emerged
and sauntered slowly into the terminal, letting the door go
behind him. Garfield crouched, wiggled, and shot—*poof!*—
like a rocket through the barest sliver (okay, *wide swath*)
of space left just before the door shut on its own. Garfield
checked that he had the room all to himself, and then
wasted no time seizing command.

He leapt onto the engineer's chair, still warm from his recent presence, and then onto the console itself. Spread
around him were monitors showing live pictures inside the
terminal, out on the platforms, and throughout the local
system. At the center of it all was a large, high-tech map of
every track in the region.

Garfield tried to make sense of the map. All of the lines
were white, and mostly straight, and didn't seem to do anything in particular. More interesting were the red dots that
appeared to coast along the lines, constantly in motion except for the occasional stop. Garfield's natural feline tracking instincts took over, and his eyes couldn't help but
follow the skittish lights hypnotically. His eyes grew heavy
and started to close, until he remembered where he was
and why he was there.

Aha! Those must be trains, stopping at remote sta-

tions. A dozen monitors, providing a glimpse into the real world, surrounded the map. Garfield could see one locomotive after another making its way across the countryside. At Garfield's feet was a dizzying selection of levers and buttons. He cracked his knuckles and prepared himself to do what he'd seen Jon do every rockin' Saturday night for more years than even Hemingway's cats could count on four paws. He found a position from which he could reach the widest possible range of controls and settled into the driver's seat, next to an empty mug that had DUANE written across it in very manly letters.

"First, you're fired," he said, slamming a paw down on the button marked AUTOPILOT. *Okay, let's light this puppy.* He used his nose and his paws to push this, pull that, and spin the other. On the map overhead, lights flashed, stopped, and otherwise broke rhythm with their previously steady beams.

I'm beginning to understand what Jon sees in all this. This is fun. The lights are so pretty. Red is a very nice color. Shows off the highlights in my coat.

A nervous voice crackled through the sound system, putting an end to Garfield's reverie. *"Control, do you read?"*

"Mostly I watch TV," Garfield replied, noticing that some of the dots were now moving toward each other along the same white line.

"It's chaos out here! Do something!" the speakers shot back. Indeed it was chaos, because out in the real world trains all over the system were now stopping, starting, backing up, and switching tracks with no apparent rhyme or reason.

Garfield pressed one control and then another. He tried

combining certain levers with particular buttons. Everything he touched only seemed to make matters worse, until there was really only one thing left to do. He put his head down on the console and covered his eyes with his paws.

The speakers roared to frantic life once more. *"This is the New Amsterdam Limited! What's going on? Why are we headed back into the station? Duane! Stop this crazy thing!"* Garfield looked up at the map. Over one route, a tiny green light blinked on and off, indicating which train had just called in. He smiled. *Once again, if you wait long enough, everything comes to you.* His confidence restored, Garfield stood on his hind legs, tucked one paw behind his back, grinned smugly, and deftly dropped an extended claw on one last well-chosen button.

The New Amsterdam Limited was inside a dark tunnel when it suddenly shrieked to a halt. In the dining car, Happy Chapman screamed when he found himself covered in the coffee that had arrived exactly to his specifications. Concerned about second-degree burns and the litigation they usually inspire, the anxious maître d' dumped an entire pitcher of ice water in Happy's steaming lap. Waiters came from every corner to blot the human volcano, who was now flailing wildly and blaming the entire affair on Wendell. This is why no one in the dining car noticed when the train reversed course and began to roll back into the station.

Garfield had already bolted from the control room and was zooming through the waiting area and under the archway just as the New York–bound train rolled to a gentle stop right back where it had started, Platform Eleven. Garfield took the stairs up two at a time and headed straight for the baggage car at the back of the train. The area was dark, with looming, wobbly stacks lining every wall.

Garfield heard a plaintive wail coming from the other side of the storage area. "Odie?" he called. "Where are you, Odie?" Garfield put his nose to the ground and followed the noise. *Finally, his weak-willed, lily-livered disposition comes in handy.*

Odie lay in his cage, as depressed a dog as ever there was, mindlessly drooling. All of a sudden, the front door to his carrier sprang open, and when Odie looked up, there was Garfield, smiling and waving.

"Look, Odie! I saved you!"

The small tan mutt with the floppy brown ears had never been so happy to see anyone in all his life. He leapt to the floor and nuzzled Garfield mightily, poking him with his nose and, of course, licking him all over.

Garfield wiped the slobber from his eyes. "Awww, stop it. Don't get all mushy."

Odie didn't relent.

"Really, it's most unbecoming."

Odie yipped and threw his two front paws joyously around Garfield's belly, and they almost met on the other side. Garfield could resist no more. He leaned his head into Odie's and nuzzled him sweetly.

"Okay, happy now?" Garfield said, breaking away and shaking himself dry. "C'mon. We've got to get off this train. There's no time to lose." They raced through the baggage car and leapt out the opening at the back.

In the dining car, Happy was yelling so loudly that the windows shook. "I want to know what is going on!" he screamed, slamming his fist down on the soggy tablecloth, which served to deaden the effect. "Why have we returned to the station?"

A quivering steward fluttered around the angry man. "Sir, would you *please* calm down!"

Wendell spotted Garfield and Odie streaking past the window. "Um, Happy?"

"What!?!" barked his supervisor.

Wendell pointed to the platform outside. Happy saw Odie and what may have been the world's fattest cat just as they gained the stairs, and he leapt to his feet. "My future is running away! I've got to get off this train!"

The conductor moved to intercept him. "Please take your seat, sir. We'll be moving again shortly."

Happy shoved the man into a table of four across the aisle, spilling water glasses and scattering dishes. "Get out of my way!" he snarled. "Something terribly wrong has happened. I've got to get off this train *right now*!"

"It's too late," said the conductor, smirking and brushing crumbs from his crisp blue uniform. "We're half out of the station. We'll start moving at any moment."

Happy barreled past the conductor like a man possessed, and general panic broke out in the dining car. All of the passengers stepped aside for the running bundle of rage as Happy tore down the aisle, darted through the exit, and jumped off the train.

Wendell turned to enjoy the rest of the show from his ringside seat by the window.

Inside the terminal, Jon argued urgently with the service representative at the information booth. "But there must be *some* way of stopping the train!" Liz paced back and forth next to him, nervously twirling her hair between her fingers.

"Hold on one moment," said the attendant. She seemed absorbed by the computer screen in front of her.

"You don't understand," Jon went on. "My cat and my dog are on that train!"

"Well, you can hold your horses, *and* your cat and your dog, while I try to figure out what's going on here," she said, distracted by the messages streaming onto her monitor.

Clear across the vaulted waiting room, Garfield and Odie burst into the area from the outdoor platform, with Happy struggling to catch up to them. As the television personality rounded the corner beyond the archway, he slammed right into a blockade of wobbling burgundy blazers. The Fraternal Order of the Raccoon Lodge was gathered to head toward their three-thirty departure, every bit as merry as they'd been on the bus ride into town.

Happy Chapman was thrown back by the wall of flesh. Perhaps it was the coffee in his eyes, or maybe he was simply deranged, but all he could see bobbing above the matching red jackets were thirty Garfields swaying atop thirty none-too-steady heads. In a heartbeat Happy was on them, yanking one hat after another to the floor.

"Hey! *What* the— Get your own hat, buster!" cried Brother Mark. In a moment all of the men were scrambling, and a melee broke out. Happy looked up to see Garfield and Odie ducking into a doorway in the side wall, next to the ticket window. By this time he was surrounded by angry Raccoons, and they were closing in fast.

Recognition seared across Happy's brain, and he now knew exactly how he was going to get out of this. "Ziggy-zaggy, ziggy-zaggy! Zug! Zug! Zug!" he shouted.

The Raccoons froze right where they were, stupefied.

"Brother!" cried Roy cheerfully.

"Ziggy-zaggy, ziggy-zaggy! Zug! Zug! Zug!" All of the Raccoons responded with their official motto and slapped each other's back boisterously. Happy seized his opportunity, slapping his way out of the throng. He bolted toward the ticket windows.

Jon and Liz couldn't help but notice the commotion that had broken out across the waiting room. They spotted Happy waving good-bye to the group of raucous gentlemen, and took off after him.

After they passed through the door, Garfield and Odie found themselves in a dark, cavernous room piled to the ceiling with suitcases, shipping cartons, and golf bags. As fast as their little legs would take them, they wove in and out of the pillars of luggage, jumping and ducking through the maze of bags.

"I think we've lost that sociopath," Garfield panted. "Let's head this way." They rounded a corner, only to see Happy hovering over them. He was holding the shock collar and sporting a lunatic grin.

"Going somewhere?" he asked, his voice casual. Happy knocked a large suitcase to the floor, blocking any route to escape.

I meant "sociopath" in the nicest possible way. Garfield and Odie cowered, wedged between a solid wall and a pile of boxes that was acting way too much like the Leaning Tower of Pisa.

"You think you can run away from Happy Chapman? No dumb, dirty animals will *ever* get the best of me!" he cried, waving the collar in menacing circles. "See how you like it with two hundred volts coursing through your thick canine head!" He lunged for Odie, twisting the fur at the back of the struggling dog's neck through white knuckles. He tried to slip the collar over his head.

Across Garfield's brain flashed the memory of Odie leaping between him and Luca, and without another thought the porcine orange cat valiantly hurled himself onto Happy's chest, shrieking and hissing for all he was worth. Happy carelessly brushed him off with one arm, sending Garfield skittering across the floor. The furry basketball only came to a stop when he thumped into a leg. He looked up to see three more just like it, and there was the pit bull he had met at the city pound.

"*Spanky?* What are you doing here?"

"Had to see it with my own eyes," Spanky replied. "A cat saving a dog." Sitting next to Spanky was Sir Simon.

"All for one, and one for all," proclaimed the former television star, shaking his kitty fist high in the air.

Garfield was utterly astonished to see thousands of cats, dogs, mice, and rats filling the baggage car. Louis stepped out from the ocean of flashing eyes and threw his shoulders back. "I say we eat the fat, arrogant fool!"

"No!" Garfield cried. "I want to live!"

"Not you, Garfield," Louis said, rolling his eyes. *"Him!"*

The animals moved in on Happy, who looked up to see himself surrounded by the advancing rabble. Their yips and growls were beginning to unnerve him. "What's going on here?" he bellowed. "I train the likes of you! I *own* the likes of you! You're not going to get the best of *me*! I'm Happy Chapman!"

Before Odie even knew what he was doing, he leaned forward and clamped his jaw down hard on Happy's fleshy calf.

"Stay still, you stupid dog!" Happy shrieked. He was just one click away from securing the shock collar around Odie's neck.

Garfield turned to the crowd and reared up on his hind legs. "Let's make him *un*-Happy Chapman!" The heroic orange tabby led the charge as all of the animals rushed to ambush the evildoer, piling themselves high until Happy was completely lost in a solid wall of fur. Arms, legs, and tails flailed in every direction.

A moment later, the mound disassembled and skittered away from the fracas. A disheveled Happy sat alone, desperately pulling at the shock collar now neatly encircling his own thick neck. He stood up and stamped his foot. Garfield sat off to the side, holding the buzzer and casually inspecting a hangnail.

"Well, Happy. Seems that the collar is on the other neck now." A big grin spread across Garfield's face as his claw came down on the button.

ZZZZAPPPP! Happy jerked and danced like popcorn in a microwave, fruitlessly grabbing at his neck.

"Look around you," Garfield continued. "There are millions out there just like us. We're no more than animals to you, but we have feelings, too." The cat was really warming to his topic, and shook a paw at the crazed man. "We want love and companionship, just like you. We live in your houses. We take your walks. We fetch your newspapers and play with your children."

The crowd murmured its vigorous agreement.

"But they don't call it the 'animal kingdom' for nothing," Garfield went on. "Don't ever forget, we ruled this planet once and we very well might rule it again someday!" A cheer welled up from the critters. Garfield noticed that the rats were by far the loudest of all, so he added: "Thousands of years ago, cats were worshipped by advanced societies. You would all do well to remember this." He stood a little taller and looked the rats hard in the eye.

"You have anything to add, Odie?" Garfield asked, turning to his grateful friend. Odie trotted over to Garfield, lifted his paw, and came down hard on the buzzer, smiling sweetly at Happy.

ZZZZAPPPP!

"Well, that about says it all, little buddy." Garfield and Odie did a joyful little dance for old times' sake, finishing with a cross-species high-five.

"This is for stealing my dog!" Jon Arbuckle strode quickly through the baggage room with Liz at his side, and—*pow!*—socked Happy right in the kisser. Chapman reeled. Before he could recover, Jon punched him one more time. "And *this* is for stealing my cat!"

Uh, Jon? Technically, he didn't steal me.

Happy crumpled into a heap on the floor, knocked out cold. Liz squealed with delight. "He ain't happy no more," she giggled.

Jon got down on one knee and threw his arms wide open, calling to the pets he'd worked so hard to find. "Garfield. Odie."

Odie bounded into Jon's arms and licked his face all over. Jon laughed and nuzzled the dog, scratching him behind the ears. They couldn't get enough of each other.

Look how happy he is to see Odie. If he loves Odie, and he loves Liz, will he still have room in his heart for me? It might be a good time to do that standoffish thing. Garfield approached Jon very tentatively.

Giddy with relief, Jon rushed on. "I was so worried

about you guys. I missed you both so much. I realized how much I love you. How much joy you bring me." He hugged Odie and looked over at Garfield. "I love being your friend, and I never want to let you out of my sight again." Jon extended a hand, beseeching his cat to join them.

With that, Garfield bounded into Jon's arms and buried his face in his chest. *You had me at "Hello."*

Liz Wilson, DVM, watched it all with a dreamy expression on her face, and pressed her hand to her heart. If there was a better man on this earth than Jon Arbuckle, certainly she had never met him.

Chapter Fifteen

Back in the suburbs, in a quaint little cul-de-sac where the tidy little houses were practically on top of each other, one gleaming platinum tabby and one overly vain Siamese sat watching the television from the sill of an open window.

"This is Walter J. Chapman We have a breaking story out of the Midwest. Abby Shields reports."

A tall woman with a microphone and really great hair stood before a chaotic crowd in front of the train station. "Thanks, Walter J. We're here at the train station where, moments ago, bedlam reigned on the New Amsterdam Limited. Apparently a deranged man went completely berserk. Unconfirmed reports indicate that it had something to do with a dog and a very heroic cat."

The camera cut from the reporter to show footage of Jon and Liz with Garfield and Odie, smiling broadly while Happy Chapman was led away in handcuffs. Happy was smiling, too, but his eyes were wild and he was babbling incomprehensibly.

"There are thousands of them! Rats and cats and dogs! They're working together against me, do y'hear? Wendell! Wendell?"

GARFIELD

With a lack of professionalism that was highly uncharacteristic of him, Walter J. Chapman blurted into his body mike, *"Good grief. That's my idiot brother!"* Happy writhed in the officers' grip.

"Ah-ah-CHOO," Happy sneezed, misting the camera lens to a soft focus.

"Garfield saved Odie," Nermal remarked, shifting his position slightly on the windowsill.

Arlene's heart swelled within her chest and she purred. "I knew he had it in him. I think he's earned pie."

Later that afternoon, Luca sat at the curb at the end of his chain, flanked by Arlene and Nermal, who had been filling the Doberman in on the day's exciting news. They watched Jon's sporty blue four-door roll up the block and turn into the Arbuckle driveway. The doors swung open and out tumbled a man, a woman, a cat, and a dog. Odie bounded toward the house, never so happy to see something in his life, and Jon turned to Liz on the front walk. He placed his hands lightly on her shoulders and looked deeply into her eyes.

"You know, Liz. Garfield and Odie mean everything to me and I couldn't have done this without you. If we hadn't found them, I could never live with myself. You're a really great friend."

Liz took a step toward Jon and looked searchingly into his face. "Jon, I want to be more than just your friend."

"Yep, really good friends are hard to come by," Jon continued. "They're a precious commodity in this world . . . What did you . . . uh, would you repeat that??"

But Liz didn't utter another word. Instead, she pulled Jon close and pressed her lips to his, kissing him passionately. And what do you know, Jon Arbuckle, the man who spent prom night organizing his sock drawer, kissed her right back. Garfield snorted and rolled his eyes.

"Now *that's* something you don't see every day," Nermal observed.

The tender scene was giving Arlene ideas. She broke from the pack and sashayed across the street toward Garfield, who was rolling on the grass and toying with a caterpillar. "I want a word with you," she said, peering down into Garfield's furry face.

The saffron feline righted himself. "It's been a long day. I'm really not in the mood, Arlene."

She locked her gaze onto his and purred saucily. "Well, *get* in the mood." Arlene let out a long, loud *"Arooooo,"* planted a big wet one right on Garfield's mouth, and didn't let go.

Garfield's golden eyes widened with shock. *What's this? Hey, this isn't bad. No nutritional value, but still—feels good! I like it!* Garfield closed his eyes and kissed her back, only twice as much.

While everyone else was lip-locked, Odie happily chased his tail on the front porch. All had met their perfect match.

A few days later, with the last of the fallen bookcase mess cleaned up and all of the "missing dog" fliers now in the recycling bin, the Arbuckle home was back to its former orderly self. Well, almost. Some things would never be the same again. Garfield and Odie sat side by side on the Sacred Chair, munching popcorn and watching a movie on television. Jon and Liz snuggled on the red velvet sofa, pretending to watch but not seeing anything except each other.

Louis sat on the windowsill outside, looking to collect on

his macadamia nut cookies and trying to get Garfield's attention without alerting the humans. Across the flickering screen scrolled the words THE END. Garfield yawned, stretched, and—*PYOYK!*—straight-armed poor Odie, who flew off the chair, landing with a bounce and a smile halfway into the kitchen, the only drool-approved floor in the house.

Garfield turned to face Louis in the window and winked. *I hate* ~~movies~~ *books with sappy endings.*

The Un-sappy End

WAKE ME
WHEN I WIN
MY OSCAR

GARFIELD
THE MOVIE

The famous fat cat
has what it takes to be a movie star:
looks, charm, and an ego the size
of the Goodyear blimp.

Putting the "wide" in wide-screen, Garfield
hogs the spotlight (and the lasagna) in his
first feature film and turns in a solid,
well-rounded performance.

Sure, like most big celebrities,
he can be a little catty, but life in the
Hollywood fat lane really suits Garfield.
As he's always said, "If you don't indulge
yourself, who will?"

GARFIELD
as himself

Garfield is the king of his cul-de-sac, but his life literally goes to the dogs when a new pet, Odie, comes into the house.

"GARFISMS"

BEWARE OF CAT!

SO LITTLE TO DO... SO MUCH TIME.

ME, ME, ME. IT'S ALL ABOUT ME!

I HATE MONDAYS.

I'M A LOVER NOT A MOUSER.

JUMP BACK! KISS MYSELF!

YOU'RE ON THE WRONG SIDE OF THE EVOLUTIONARY CURVE.

COVER ME, POOKY. I'M GOING IN.

ODIE man's best friend

Cute, lovable, but a few dog biscuits shy of a box—that's Odie. All Odie wants is to become part of the family, but can Garfield share his owner—and his favorite chair—with this dopey dog?

BRECKIN MEYER
as Jon

Jon Arbuckle is Garfield's mild-mannered owner. Can he get a date with Liz the vet— and keep a certain oversize orange tabby from devouring all the pasta in the house?

DOG MISSING

"ODIE"

- LIGHT BROWN WITH DARK BROWN EARS & PAWS

JENNIFER LOVE HEWITT
as Liz

Liz Wilson is a young, attractive veterinarian with an obvious weakness for dumb, helpless animals (like Odie . . . and Jon Arbuckle).

DEBRA MESSING
as Arlene

Garfield's sassy gal pal. Unfortunately, Garfield's more interested in feeding his face than finding true love.

DAVID EIGENBERG

as Nermal

A simpleminded cat who worships the ground Garfield waddles on.

STEPHEN TOBOLOWSKY
as Happy Chapman

Seemingly good-natured TV spokesman (along with his cat, Persnikitty) for Kibbly Cat Food. But Happy isn't what he appears to be and hatches a plot to kidnap Odie. Can Garfield save the day (and his pooch pal)?

as Walter Chapman

Happy's brother and a news anchorman. He has everything Happy wants: success, respect, and a full head of hair.

TV host Christopher Mello (left) with Happy Chapman and Persnikitty (right).

DID YOU KNOW?
Garfield Movie Trivia

RELAX, I'M IN CHARGE HERE

GARFIELD

* Stephen Tobolowsky has appeared in more than eighty movies.

* Odie is actually played by two dogs: brother and sister Tyler and Chloe.

* In 1982, at the age of eight, Breckin Meyer was a cast member on the TV game show *Child's Play*.

* Jim Davis's favorite movie is *Airplane!* ("Love those fighting Girl Scouts!")

* Peter Hewitt wrote, produced, and directed the 2002 British film *Thunderpants*.

* Debra Messing (Arlene) won an Emmy for her TV show in 2003.

* The character Christopher Mello was named in honor of a Garfield fan who died in the World Trade Center on September 11, 2001.

* Jennifer Love Hewitt's first major screen role was in Disney's *Kids Incorporated* (1984). She was five years old.

* Animation supervisor Chris Bailey was an animator on Disney's *The Little Mermaid* and directed several episodes of *Kim Possible*.

* While they share the same last name, Garfield creator Jim Davis and producer John Davis are not related.

CREW

Garfield demands nothing but the best, so Twentieth Century Fox called in some Hollywood heavyweights to take care of the cat.

Producing the movie is Davis Entertainment, which has been responsible for such comedies as *Doctor Dolittle* and *Doctor Dolittle 2, Grumpy Old Men*, and *Daddy Day Care*. The production team includes Neil Machlis (executive producer), John Davis, head of Davis Entertainment (producer), and Brian Manis (coproducer).

Who's the top dog on Garfield's movie set? Director Peter Hewitt, who's been at the helm of such family favorites as *The Borrowers* and Disney's *Tom and Huck*.

And keeping the fat cat lookin' good is director of photography Dean Cundey, who's no stranger to oversize animal stars. His films include *Who Framed Roger Rabbit?* and *Jurassic Park*.

THREE MEN AND A CAT: On the set with (left to right) Dean Cundey, Peter Hewitt, and John Davis.

Filming on *Garfield* began March 10, 2003. More than two hundred people worked on the project—actors, technicians, costume designers, makeup artists, set decorators, builders, electricians, cameramen, caterers—all helping to create movie magic.

DREAM TEAM:
The cast and crew of Garfield.

FROM THE COMICS PAGE...

It all started June 19, 1978, when a certain fat cat sauntered onto the comics page. Twenty-five years later, *Garfield* is the most widely syndicated comic strip in history, appearing in more than 2,500 newspapers around the world.

Having conquered books and TV, the famous feline was ready to sink his teeth into the movies. Keeping enough lasagna on the set was tough!

"What makes Garfield so popular? People relate to him because he is them. After all, Garfield is really a human in a cat suit."

—Jim Davis,
Garfield creator

...TO THE SILVER SCREEN

"We found a character that encompassed all we believed in. Laziness. Food. More food. The French call it 'raison d'etre.' We call it 'freedom fries.'"

—Alec Sokolow and
Joel Cohen, writers

A great movie starts with a great script, and the studio found the perfect writers to capture Garfield's unique, larger-than-life "purr-sonality": Alec Sokolow and Joel Cohen, cowriters of *Toy Story*, the monster hit of 1995. To work on the Garfield movie, Alec and Joel flew out to Muncie, Indiana, and spent a week brainstorming with Jim Davis. They went back to Hollywood fully "Garfieldized," and the movie practically wrote itself.

"It's quite something to be entrusted with making such a well-loved character fully dimensional for the cinema screen. The one thing I was determined to do was to make sure that even though our cat was real, organic, photo-realistic and totally alive in each frame, he was also 100% Garfield. So the more complex and technical the process got, the more we went back to that cheeky little cat in the strip to find our answers.

—Peter Hewitt, director

Peter Hewitt and Jim Davis with an early version of the Garfield puppet.

Detailed drawings of some sequences were created to help the director and his effects team visualize Garfield's movements. These sketches also helped determine the best way to stage and shoot a scene.

The full-size Garfield puppet was created as a stand-in for the computer-generated image, which was added later.

INVISIBLE CAT?

In some instances, the actors didn't use the puppet but merely pretended to interact with Garfield. Animators then took this footage and digitally added the computer image.

LEFT: The pet-dancing scene is filmed with the Garfield puppet and a toy dog representing Odie. Boogie, oogie, oogie!

RIGHT: The scene in which Garfield escapes from Luca is also filmed using the puppet and doll stand-ins.
BELOW: Directing the wake-up scene, Peter Hewitt flings the Garfield puppet at a cringing Breckin. Heads up!

THE ART OF BEING GARFIELD

Bringing Garfield from the two-dimensional world of the comic strip to the three-dimensional world of film was quite a challenge. Jim Davis, his artists, and the Fox production people worked like dogs to create the cat's movie look. Here are some early concept sketches and sculpts that show Garfield's evolution.

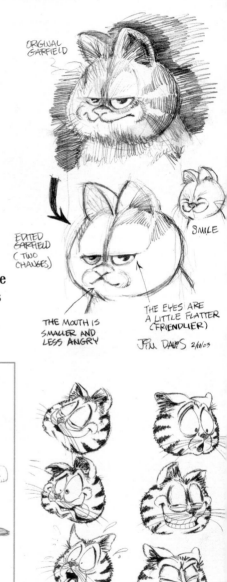

ORIGINAL GARFIELD

SMILE

EDITED GARFIELD (TWO CHANGES)

THE MOUTH IS SMALLER AND LESS ANGRY

THE EYES ARE A LITTLE FLATTER (FRIENDLIER)

JIM DAVIS 2/11/03

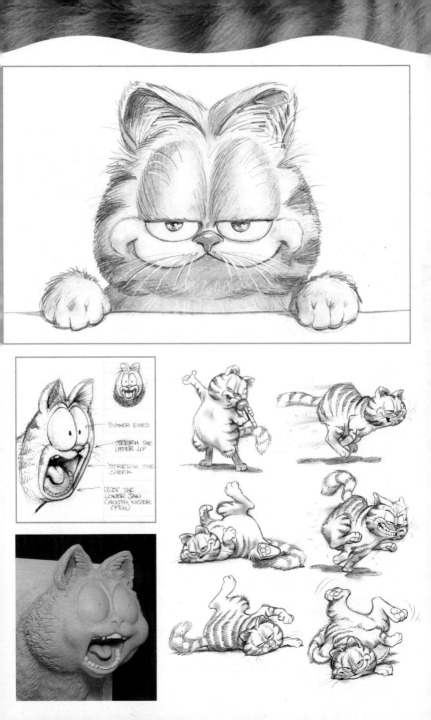

BIGGER EYES

STRETCH THE
UPPER LIP

STRETCH THE
CHEEK

DROP THE
LOWER JAW
(MOUTH WIDER
OPEN)

COMPUTER CAT

Visual effects supervisor Dan DeLeeuw (left) and animation director Chris Bailey (right) work their CGI magic.

While the other four-legged characters in the film are portrayed by actual animals, Garfield is a computer-generated image (or CGI, as it's known in the industry).

That's right: The flabby feline is animated completely in the computer. How does a computer-generated image move and act like a real animal? All it takes is an army of artists, enough computer hardware to launch the space shuttle, and a few million dollars. Simple, huh?

There are only a few companies that can do CGI right, and Garfield was fortunate to get one of the best in the biz: Rhythm & Hues. R&H has done digital effects for *Scooby-Doo, Stuart Little, The Cat in the Hat, Doctor Dolittle 2,* and a zillion other big films.

CGI is an extremely time- and labor-intensive process, and it can take animators literally months to create material that will fill only a few minutes of screen time.

The task of creating the digital Garfield fell to animation supervisor Chris Bailey. During principal photography, Chris was on the set every day (and often long into the night), working with the director on Garfield's expressions and movements.

Once shooting wrapped, Chris set up shop at Rhythm & Hues, where he and more than two hundred animators, artists, and technicians spent several months getting Garfield ready for his big-screen debut.

STAGES OF THE CGI PROCESS:

1 Pencil sketch

2 Animated model without hair

3 The final fuzzy phenomenon!

ANIMAL ANTICS

Never trust a smiling cat.

CAT BURGLAR:
Nermal pilfers the pie.

FOTO FUN

PETER IS SO GOOD AT TAKING DIRECTION!

Producer Brian Manis sneaks on-screen as the tailor.

GOOD BOY! Now go fetch a pizza!

LIP SERVICE
Jennifer gets gussied up for the camera.

PEEKABOO!
We're ready for our close-ups!

JENNIFER LOVE HEWITT

GARFIELD

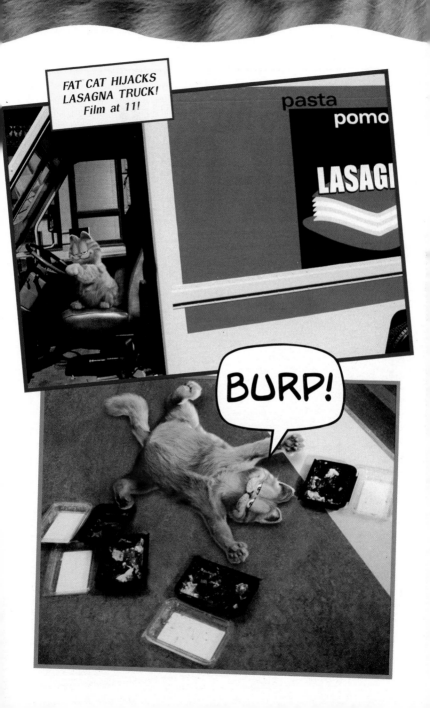

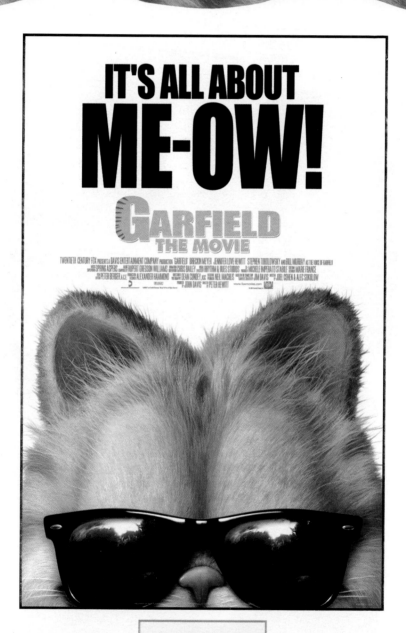

The movie poster!